City of Brotherly Mayhem

Philadelphia
Crimes & Criminals

By RON AVERY

Otis Books
Philadelphia

———— Dedicated to: ————

Serge and Ben Avery

Two fine sons.
Two good Philadelphians.

OTIS BOOKS
Philadelphia, 1997
Second Printing, 2003

Cover Design by Hoffman Studio
Cover Photo: Sam Psoras
Text Design: Eric J. Eklund
Printer: George H. Buchanan Company, Philadelphia

Library of Congress Catalog Number: 97-91942

ISBN 0-9658825-0-0

City of Brotherly Mayhem

Philadelphia Crimes & Criminals

CONTENTS

PHILADELPHIA. It's Greek and means brotherly love.

Over the years boosters have labeled Philadelphia: The Quaker City. The Cradle of Liberty. The Athens of America. Workshop of the World. City of Homes. City of Firsts.

All are relatively accurate; so is City of Brotherly Mayhem.

Crime, vice, murder, riots, corruption, lawlessness and violence are integral to any serious consideration of the city's 315-year history.

Crime arrived with the first ships. A year after William Penn established his "Holy Experiment" in 1682, he found it necessary to set up a whipping post. Six years later, the benevolent founder wrote in despair of the drunkenness, prostitution, gambling and crime that reigned on the riverfront.

By the 1690s the city's Quakers were so bitterly divided over the preaching of a certain George Keith that the sacred tenet of pacifism was forgotten as the two factions battled with fists.

The obnoxious behavior of Penn's foppish son Billy sparked a barroom free-for-all, a challenge to a duel and a bill of indictment against Billy and his friends for assault.

Not to pick on the generally peaceful, industrious Quakers. Even those proper Anglicans at Christ Church came to blows and invitations to duel when a new pastor in 1715 reportedly boasted of his sexual conquest of young ladies in the congregation. Half the parishioners felt the Rev. Francis Phillips had been grievously libeled; others were ready to string-up the scoundrel.

The theme continues throughout the 18th century: minor riots in 1726 and 1738, sailors hired to crack skulls in the bloody election of 1742, setting a precedent (as we shall see in Chapters 2 and 5) of election mayhem extending into the 20th century.

Probably no Colonial American city had more taverns and grog shops, legal and illicit. Washington and Jefferson may have taken their tankard of ale at sedate City Tavern, but the rabble congregated in the taprooms and vice dens along three blocks of Race Street known as "Helltown."

Lawlessness and mayhem reached a crescendo during the middle decades of the 19th century. Criminal gangs ruled entire neighborhoods. Some volunteer fire companies were little more than warring gangs. Anti-Catholic (actually anti-Irish) riots in the summer of 1844 left two Catholic churches and several blocks of homes in ashes and at least a dozen dead. At one point, rioters and the militia blasted away at each other with cannons. Major anti-black riots erupted every few years during the same period.

The early decades of the 20th century found the city mired in outrageous political corruption and labor violence that reached their peak with 29 deaths during the 66-day trolley strike of 1910. In more recent times, Philadelphia's image in the national consciousness has been shaped, in large part, by the likes of John Africa, Gary Heidnik, John DuPont, Nicky Scarfo and Eddie Savitz. For years a frequently asked question of Philadelphia tour guides was, "Where is that neighborhood that your mayor bombed?"

This book explores 15 of Philadelphia's most sensational crimes and interesting criminals. Fifteen chapters was simply an arbitrary number chosen at the start of the project. Fifty would have been a more realistic figure. What a marvelous abundance!

"You mean you're not including Elmo Smith?" asked an incredulous friend. No. And simply for reasons of space, I have skipped Jack Lopinson and Ethel Kravitz and Ira Einhorn and a dozen other worthy and interesting cases. I have also decided to bypass stories that are still fresh in the memories of most Philadelphians. The Mafia Wars of the 1980s have been well documented. Most people recall the fascinating details of the disappearance of teacher Susan Reinert and her children and the stomach-churning crimes perpetrated in "Reverend" Heidnik's "House of Horrors."

The book is organized in chronological order, starting with the massacre of the Deering Family in 1866 and ending with the titillating John Knight III murder case of 1975.

My primary objective in writing this book is the simple wish that readers will find these tales interesting reading. Secondarily, I hope the book imparts something of the flavor of the times and stimulates interest in Philadelphia's rich history.

Now to acknowledge the many kind people who offered help and advice. It will soon become obvious that the source for the bulk of the book was gleaned from the endless reading of old newspapers. Sincere thanks to the helpful, cheerful staff of the Inquirer–Daily News research library. Special thanks to the ever-patient Frank Donahue.

I spent nearly as much time in the Urban Archives of Temple University's Paley Library. This matchless resource is the final resting place for the records of many Philadelphia institutions and the news clippings and photo files of the defunct Evening Bulletin. A special tip of the beanie to the Archive's George D. Brightbill, who put me on the trail of the 1930s Arsenic Ring and the skull-bashing politics of "The Bloody Fifth Ward." Thanks, too, to head archivist Margaret J. Jerrido and assistants Brenda Galloway–Wright and Cheryl Johnson.

Heaps of gratitude to the that warm and generous historian–educator Harry Silcox for his encouragement and sharing of his material on Octavius Catto. Thanks to Phil Lapsanksy of The Library Company for sharing his vast knowledge of city history.

A gracious bow to grizzled Daily News reporters Joe Daughen and Dave Racher, for sharing memories. A special thank–you to Sam Psoras, the retired dean of Philadelphia news photographers, for the use of the charming photo that graces the cover. Many thanks to Jim Anderson, Charlie Field and Harold Franklin for advice on the publishing game. And a Ten-Four to two of the nicest retired Philadelphia lawmen you'll ever meet, private-eye Bill Fleisher and fearless bounty-hunter Jim Kelly.

Blessings upon the creative noggin of Joanne Hoffman for her cover design. Deepest and most sincere thanks to editor-in-chief Maryanne Furia for translating my slanguage into standard English and unerringly catching every ridiculous spelling error.

Finally, a few words of praise for three marvelous Philadelphians who have sadly passed away in recent years. It was my privilege to know (briefly) and be inspired (greatly) by Max Whiteman, John Francis Marion and Arthur H. Lewis.

They were historian–writers. Each was an impeccable researcher. Unencumbered by the deadening conventions of academia, this trio brought Philadelphia history and personalities to vibrant life. I am just arrogant enough to hope that this book will continue their remarkable legacy to Philadelphia and its history.

Ron Avery

Ax-Murderer Anton Probst.

CHAPTER 1

Eight Dead in The Neck!
Anton Probst

As late as 1919, writer Christopher Morley described the South Philadelphia district known as "The Neck" in lyric terms: "Green meadows lie under pink sunset light. . . . In the stable yards horses stand munching at barn doors. A girl in a faded blue pinafore comes up the road leading two white horses; a solitary cow trails along behind."

The Neck—basically everything south of Moore Street—was even more bucolic in 1866 when the sleepy farming community became the scene of the most horrendous crime in city history—at least to that point.

The attention of the entire city was focused on the farm of Christopher Deering on Jones Lane where the bodies of seven people were found on April 11. An eighth victim would be discovered the next day. All had their throats cut—hacked would be a better description—and their skulls horribly smashed and mutilated. Four of those slaughtered were small children—the youngest a 14-month-old infant.

There was no public transportation to The Neck in 1866, but throngs rushed to the scene. Here's the way one reporter described it: "Thousands of persons journeyed from the upper parts of Philadelphia to gratify their morbid curiosity. . . . We were surprised to see the vast number of persons on foot walking or running as if it were a race of life and death. There were old men who would not have to travel far to find their graves, and hundreds of young men, who were making a holiday excursion of the fearful pilgrimage. A minister of the gospel on horseback passed us, trotting rapidly along. A cripple on crutches swung his distorted legs over the dusty road, making no slow progress. But the women outnumbered the men of all ages, and in all attires from the fashionably dressed lady in her barouche to the poor seamstress on foot."

At the site, police kept the crowd from entering the ransacked Deering Farmhouse. But the mob pushed into the barn and corncrib where neighbors had found the ghastly remains of Deering; his wife, Julia; the bodies of four of their five children; and Deering's 25-year-old cousin, Elizabeth Dolan. Only the bloody straw remained to satisfy the curious. The bodies had been removed to a funeral home in Center City for autopsies. The police had confiscated the ax, the hatchet and a hammer believed to be the murder weapons.

The gruesome discovery was made by neighbor Abraham Everett whose farm was about a quarter-mile distant. He had last seen activity on the Deering spread on Saturday, April 7. By Wednesday, curiosity got the better of Everett and he paid a visit. He found the house locked. In the barn, two horses, a pig and cattle tied in their stalls were near death from lack of water and feed.

As the good neighbor watered and fed the animals, he saw a foot protruding from a hay pile on the barn floor. He rushed to get others who returned and found the bloody, decomposing bodies of Deering and his cousin lying side-by-side.

Police under Chief Detective Benjamin Franklin (not to be confused with the electrician) rushed to the farm. Attached to the side of the barn was a box-like corncrib. Heaped together inside were the cadavers of Julia Deering and her four youngsters: John, 8; Thomas, 6; Anna, 4; and the infant Emily. Ten-year-old William, called "Willie," had been visiting with grandparents and thus escaped the slaughter to continue the family name, which the press sometimes spelled "Dearing."

The next day newspapers blared the tale of "a frightful tragedy in the First Ward." The Bulletin said suspicion falls on "a lad called Cornelius, 17 years old, who was bound to Mr. Dearing; and a hired man living with him, a German whose name none of the residents thereabouts could give."

Mayor Morton McMichael immediately advertised a $1,000 reward for "information that shall lead to the detection and conviction of the perpetrator or perpetrators of this most horrible deed."

The next morning the teen-aged hand was eliminated as a suspect when police searching the farm found the body of Cornelius Carey hidden inside a tall haystack about 300 yards from the barn. He, too, died like the others: his skull horribly smashed, his throat slashed from ear-to-ear.

There was now a description of the German farmhand: about 30, muscular, bull-necked, missing his right thumb. His English was poor, and his first name was believed to be "Anthony."

That same Thursday evening "Anthony" was captured, and policeman James Dorsey became the hero of the hour. Dorsey, in the company of two other cops, spotted a suspicious character with his hat pulled low over his face approaching the Market Street Bridge to West Philly. And Dorsey also noticed the man was missing a thumb. The officer lifted the suspect's hat for a better look and asked, "You are a Dutchman?" The stranger's answer became famous: "No, me are a Frenchman."

The cops were pretty sure they had their man and locked him up in a police station on Filbert Street. The next morning word spread of the arrest and a mob appeared, threatening quick justice. The first newspaper editions gave the suspect's name as "Antione Ganter." Anton Probst turned out to be a lousy liar.

The distraught mother of murdered Elizabeth Dolan identified the prisoner as the hired hand. He had worked for Christopher Deering in the fall, quit, but reappeared a few weeks ago. The cattle farmer felt sorry for the penniless immigrant and rehired Probst at $10 a month plus board until he could find another position. The newspapers reported that Mrs. Deering had always felt uneasy about the sullen, brutish foreigner.

A search of Probst's clothing turned up items, including a snuffbox and a pistol, which belonged to the murdered farmer. In fact, the clothes and boots that Probst wore also belonged to his former employer.

On Friday morning Mayor McMichael, who had been county sheriff during the bloody anti-Catholic riots of 1844, questioned the prisoner. A German-speaking aide assisted, and the interview was taken down and printed in the newspapers.

The suspect's muttered answers were a monosyllabic mishmash of truth and lies. Probst admitted killing farmhand Cornelius Carey, but said the other seven slayings were the bloody work of an acquaintance. He identified his accomplice as "Jacob Gaunter" or "Yonder." Probst had served in the recently concluded American Civil War and the murderous Gaunter, a Swiss, was in the same unit.

By now police knew that Christopher Deering had gone off in a buggy early Saturday morning to transact business and to pick up Elizabeth Dolan who would arrive by steamboat from Burlington, N.J., where she had been visiting other relatives. This left Probst and Carey alone on the farm with Mrs. Deering and the four children. Probst said he commenced the slaughter by killing his co-worker as they worked in a field. His war buddy then killed the mother and children. When the farmer and Miss Dolan arrived in the afternoon, the diabolical Gaunter dispatched the pair.

Probst admitted to being drunk the night before the murders and on the morning of the massacre. Following the slaughter, the pair went into the farmhouse, had a bite to eat and searched for cash. Probst said Gaunter found several hundred dollars but gave him only $3. The pair departed about 7 p.m., going separate ways with vague plans to meet again on Front Street. Probst said he simply wandered about the city and South Jersey for the next five days until his capture.

"Did you not think somebody would be after you for doing these things?" asked the mayor. The prisoner muttered, "I guessed it would be all right when you'd catch me."

Question: "You did not care to get away?" Answer: "No."

Question: "You never thought of killing these people until the man suggested it to you?" Answer: "No."

Question: "Mr. Deering always treated you very kindly? You had no quarrel with him?" Answer, "No."

A mob of some 2,000 "yelling and hooting" citizens waited on the street; a line of policemen stretching two blocks prevented a lynching as a police van rushed Probst at the gallop to the safety of Moyamensing Prison.

In the meanwhile, a coroners' jury was going about its grim task. While police kept back those who gathered in front of Cyrus Horn's funeral home at 11th and Filbert, a certain Dr. Shapleigh minutely examined the well-iced bodies, one by one. Every horrible wound, gash, tear and cut was measured and noted. The report was published in the newspapers, providing a stomach-churning trove of gruesome details.

Funerals for all eight victims were held on Saturday; the rites amazingly included an open-casket viewing. "The bodies were shrouded in white and all that art could do to soften the ghastly appearance of the fatal wounds had been done. In order to prevent access to the house by unauthorized persons a posse of police was stationed on the steps and all who claimed the right of admission were required to present a ticket showing their claim to be genuine," said a paperback account of the murders rushed into print after the crime.

The horse-drawn funeral cortege wound its way through city streets lined with solemn-faced citizens to St. Mary's Cemetery in South Philadelphia. "A large concourse of persons" assembled in the burial grounds as a Catholic priest sprinkled the coffins with holy water and offered the appropriate prayers.

On Monday the coroner's jury held a four-hour hearing. "The prisoner was present during the entire investigation and did not manifest the slightest feeling from beginning to end. Not even when the bloody instruments with which the horrible murders were committed were displayed and the terrible wounds inflicted described did he move a muscle," wrote the anonymous paperback author.

Various items found in Probst's possession or sold by the suspect were identified as coming from the Deering home. Probst's bloody clothes, found in the farmhouse, were identified. A bartender and a prostitute remembered Probst showing them two pocket watches and two pistols after the murders.

There was debate, but the evidence plus the many inconsistent and false statements by Probst pointed to the fact that he acted alone. Many doubted that one man alone could have killed eight people. Others argued that no two people could be so wantonly cruel and bloodthirsty. And the press declared the 24-year-old Probst to be a "solitary, morose man without acquaintances and friends."

In the end, authorities decided Probst acted alone. For some technical reason he was tried only for the murder of Christopher Deering. A jury began hearing testimony on April 26, just 15 days after the bodies were found. Lawyers John P. O'Neill and John A. Wolbert were appointed to defend the sullen German; neither was thrilled by the assignment. Directing the prosecution was District Attorney William B. Mann, who would author a book on the case.

In Mann's powerful opening address he characterized the defendant as "a cruel and brutal wretch, some monster of iniquity [who] entered the threshold of a humble dwelling in a secluded neighborhood with one fell purpose and murdered a whole family. . . . including the very infant in the cradle. . . . Indeed gentleman, no one incident of the atrocities has envenomed the popular fury against the ruffian so much as the useless butchery on this infant. Was there no pity in the heart of the wretch? No shudder there as he deliberately took the pure innocent babe from its cradle and brained it whilst smiling in her face?"

The prosecution then presented a reading of the eight grisly autopsies. The only surviving Deering—10-year-old Willie—identified the ax and his father's two watches. The bulk of the testimony came from those who had contact with Probst in the days between the murders and his capture. He spent the first night with a harlot, at a cost of $3. Most of the remaining time was spent in drinking beer and playing cards in a saloon-boarding house on New Market Street in North Liberties, known as "Leckfeldt's." He was in Leckfeldt's when someone read aloud an account of the murders in a German-language newspaper. Everyone, including Probst, agreed it was horrifying and a disgrace that a German was the suspect.

Police and detectives entered the saloon but didn't recognize the suspect. Probst's statement said his accomplice took Deering's gold-plated watch. But a jeweler positively identified Probst as the man who sold him the same timepiece.

There were no witnesses for the defense. In his closing argument, defense attorney Wolbert cautioned jurors not to convict on circumstantial evidence. No one could say for sure when the victims were slain. The slayings might have been committed well after Probst departed on Saturday night. And if the defendant was truly guilty, why didn't he flee the city?

"We are not to try by theory but by evidence," said the lawyer. "Look on those eight bodies and say if one man could have done that. . . . I submit, gentlemen, theories won't do; it must be facts submitted to you. Eight people murdered and all by one man!"

It took the jury only two hours to return with a guilty verdict. The judge swiftly sentenced the villain to die on the gallows. And the governor wasted no time signing the death warrant.

The most brutal and shocking Philadelphia murder case of the 19th century might have become mired in the endless debate and speculation about accomplices—casting Probst in the role of an early-American Lee Harvey Oswald. But history was spared such conspiracy theories when the uncommunicative killer, under the influence of a kindly priest, opened up and made a full confession in preparation of that final judgment.

On May 7, Rev. P. A.M Grundtner of St. Alphonsus' Church, 4th and Reed, informed authorities that Probst was ready to talk. His two defense attorneys, Detective Ben Franklin, and prison officials took his confession. Later the press was allowed into his cell to hear the same story from the chained prisoner.

"Anton Probst threw off the impassibility of feature that had always characterized him before the public and showed more of the inner thoughts and motives than one could have dared to hope. He spoke in a low tone with a German accent and idiom . . . .Often his hands played mechanically with the separate beads of the rosary," wrote DA Mann. And according to Mann's account, Probst sometimes smiled when relating details of the massacre.

By way of background, Probst said he was a native of Uehlingen in Baden, who arrived in New York on May 9th, 1863. Two hours after landing, he enlisted in a New York infantry regiment, which carried an immediate cash bonus. He deserted six weeks later, in Washington. He apparently enlisted and deserted from a second New York unit. The murderer finished out a third enlistment in Pennsylvania's 5th Cavalry where he managed to accidentally shoot his thumb off.

After the war, the brawny German took a job in a Philadelphia sugar refinery, but found the work too hot. He bounced around the region, spending time in Philadelphia's Blockley Almshouse. In late fall 1866, he spent three weeks working on the Deering farm. He quit when Deering asked him to work outside on "a rainy, very rough day."

He returned to the Deering farm in March 1866. "I knew he had money in the house. I had seen him counting money. I had not thought of committing murder at the time but I calculated to rob him of money. . . .I planned every day to get the money but never got a chance; I never thought of murder until the day I murdered them." In fact, Deering, a 38-year-old Irishman, didn't have much money. He leased his farm from a city man who also put up the cash for livestock. Deering's profits were split with the businessman.

Probst said on the day Deering left for the city, "I formed the design to murder the entire family." He was working in a pasture with Cornelius. As the youth rested under a tree, casually chatting about work, Probst struck him from behind with the ax and used the same ax to cut the boy's throat.

Probst wiped the blood off with straw and hid the body in the haystack. He returned to the stable where he lured eight-year-old John Deering into the barn, saying he needed help. Again, Probst attacked from behind with the ax. The boy fell without a sound. Probst placed the body in the corn-crib.

Next, Probst knocked on the door of the farmhouse and told Mrs. Deering he was having a problem in the barn with one of the horses and needed her help. He waited for her arrival in the gloom. "She comes in the stable. I stood inside and struck her on the head; she did not holler. I gave her two or three more blows and chopped her throat."

Next Probst told Thomas, 6, that his mother wanted him in the barn and promptly murdered the child in the same fashion. He returned to the house and took Annie, 4, and the baby into the barn. He let the infant play in the hay while he murdered Annie and then dispatched the infant.

Shortly after 1 p.m. Deering returned in the buggy with his cousin. The young woman took her suitcase into the house, and Probst approached the farmer, declaring that one of the steers in the barn was very ill. Deering rushed into the barn to have a look. Probst followed behind. The two axes were waiting in a corner. "I walked behind him and hit him right on the head with the small ax. He fell right down on his face. I turned him over and gave him one or two more on his head and cut his throat."

Finally, Probst summoned the young woman into the barn. On the way she asked where Mrs. Deering and children were. Probst allegedly smiled recalling his reply: "They're in the barn." He used the hammer to knock down the woman, and the ax to finish her off.

With the slaughter complete, Probst searched the farmhouse. He said he found a total of $17. He shaved with his victim's razor, ate some bread and butter and changed into Deering's clothes.

"After I killed the first boy I did not care if a hundred were there; if a hundred had gone there I would have killed them all without caring. I do not know why I felt that way. I had no feeling against the family, only I wanted the money. They always treated me well." Probst said he killed the infant because he was afraid the child would cry.

Confession proved good for the soul of Anton Probst. Though he had quaked with fear when the mob threatened to pull him to pieces earlier, he now accepted his impending hanging with calm resolve. He ate and slept well, wrote a note of thanks to his lawyers and a farewell letter to his parents in Germany.

One newspaper had expressed fears that Probst's thick neck might make his execution difficult. That worry was not necessary. On June 8, the excellent Moyamensing Prison gallows performed its task perfectly. Wrote Mann: "Never in our observation did nature more easily cease its strife. The neck was probably broken at the first shock. There was a natural convulsive shudder of the frame, but the murderer was dead within three minutes of the drop."

The body was donated to Jefferson Medical School where a plaster cast was made of Probst's head and his skeleton prepared for display in the school's museum. But first, wrote Mann, there were some interesting experiments: "The opportunity was a very rare one to verify the truth of the theory that upon the retina of the eye of one who dies a sudden death is imprinted, as by photography, the image of the last object upon which it rests. The last face that met the gaze of the prisoner was the sad, kind face of Sheriff [Henry] Howell."

Would Probst's dead eyes reveal a snapshot of the dear old sheriff? An examination with an "ophthalmoscope lit by a powerful electric light" showed only blood and "mucous discharge."

Then the Jefferson professors proceeded to perform a number of "galvanic" experiments on the body with electricity. Finally, writes Mann, "A surgeon took out the right eye and secured it in a bottle. It was an interesting specimen of a ruptured pupil."

According to later news stories, no one wanted to live on the Deering Farmhouse because of its horrific history. It remained empty and eventually burned down. The site is now the Food Distribution Center, not far from the Walt Whitman Bridge. Survivor Willie Deering was raised by his maternal grandparents in their West Philadelphia butcher shop. He is said to have married and fathered seven children, two of whom died in infancy.

There are still Deering descendants in the region, but the family graves disappeared when the cemetery at 10th and Moore was cleared for construction of Saint Maria Goretti High School in the 1950s. Anton Probst's skeleton at Jefferson was discarded or misplaced decades ago.

Octavius Catto was slain during the bloody election riots of 1871.

CHAPTER 2

An Election Day Murder
Octavius Catto

There was nothing particularly unusual about white mobs attacking Philadelphia's black citizens during the 19th century, but the 1871 Election Day riots were shocking because among those left dead on the sidewalk was Octavius V. Catto.

Catto was sort of a local Jesse Jackson/Colin Powell/Jackie Robinson rolled into one dynamic figure. He was young, handsome, highly-educated, articulate, bold and a natural leader.

He was the boys' principal of the Institute for Colored Youth, a nationally renowned school for blacks—a place whose "scholars" by mastering Greek, Latin, English composition and higher mathematics astonished whites and filled every black Philadelphian with pride.

Catto was also the captain and star player of The Pythians, an all-black baseball team, undefeated in 1867. Of course, white teams refused to play the Pythians or permit any black teams into their leagues. He helped recruit an African-American company for the Pennsylvania National Guard during the Civil War and rose to major, a rare black in the officer ranks. At the time of his death, he was a high-ranking member of the all-black Fifth Brigade, First Division, Pennsylvania National Guard.

He was a victorious leader in the first civil rights battle fought by Philadelphia's blacks: the right to ride on horse-drawn streetcars. Some of the same non-violent tactics employed 100 years later in the black civil rights movement were pioneered by Catto, including mass arrests of blacks who boarded streetcars. He was a leader in several black cultural and political organizations and had ties to important white politicians and civic leaders.

Octavius Catto might have become a national figure. He was known in Washington and had been offered a federal position in educating newly-freed slaves. He might have become the first Philadelphia African-American elected to political office—a city councilman, a state legislator. Who knows how high this talented man might have climbed?

But at age 32, the promising, young leader was assassinated. It happened on Election Day, November 10, 1871. He was shot down just a few feet from his rooming house on the sidewalk of South Street near 9th. It happened on a crowded street in broad daylight. Three other black men and a white were slain and scores of blacks and whites injured in racial fighting sparked by the election. But it was the brazen, senseless slaying of a promising black leader which makes the riots memorable.

To understand what happened in November 1871, it helps to know that city government was in Democratic hands, but their hold was shaky; the Republican Party was poised to take control. In 1871 blacks would naturally vote for the GOP, "The Party of Lincoln." It wasn't until Franklin Roosevelt's New Deal that African-American voters switched political allegiance.

Voting was an exciting novelty to local blacks in 1871. In 1835, the Pennsylvania legislature had disenfranchised blacks, pure bigotry being the sole motive. However, the 15th Amendment guaranteeing the vote to all (males) regardless of color or "previous condition of servitude" became law in 1870. Although there were no important local races in 1870, blacks turned out in large numbers—standing in separate lines at the polls. A company of Marines was dispatched by a federal magistrate to maintain order in Southwark and Moyamensing, where many blacks were expected to vote and where Election Day violence was common. But the day passed calmly.

Catto was organizing black voters for the Republican Party in a neighborhood where it was dangerous to be black *or* Republican. The black population was concentrated in Southwark; Moyamensing; and the blocks between Pine and South, 5th and 8th streets. Still, they were a minority living cheek-by-jowl with thousands of poor, unfriendly Irish Catholics. One narrow alley might be all-black and the next Irish.

The political boss of the neighborhood was Democrat "Squire" William McMullen, a colorful political fixer known for his generosity to supporters and the liberal use of street violence. Many of his violence-prone supporters were members of Moyamensing Hose Company. The city was in the process of disbanding scores of volunteer fire companies that were often little more than street gangs organized on political and ethnic lines. Moyamensing Hose belonged to McMullen and his Irish toughs.

The Squire was a bigot and black-baiter who fought to keep blacks off the streetcars. When one line decided to open its cars to black riders and to poll whites on the experiment, McMullen schemed to influence opinion by paying two black cesspool cleaners to ride the line in their most fragrant work clothes. A couple of the Squire's toughs accompanied the pair to make sure they rode to the end of the line.

There's little doubt that McMullen was the instigator of the Election Day race riots of 1871. He would eventually appear as an alibi witness at the trials of those charged with the worst acts of violence. The two men eventually tried for the murder of Catto wore the tattoo of the Moyamensing Hose—the number "27" on the backs of their hands. (Moyamensing was the 27th fire company chartered in the city.) The triggerman worked as a bartender in the saloon next-door to the firehouse.

Violence erupted three days before the election with attacks on blacks sparking several warm-up, brick-tossing donnybrooks. Several blacks were shot. Jacob Gordon, the first fatality, was shot dead near 8th and Bainbridge for no apparent reason but intimidation.

On Election Day the fighting broke out in the morning in front of a polling place at 6th and Lombard. It wasn't only white toughs who were attacking blacks waiting to vote: the police were just as active in discouraging men of color from entering the polls. In those pre-Civil Service days the cops were all loyal Democratic hacks; a GOP victory would mean unemployment.

After the riots, Jacob C. White Jr., a black educator and the last person Catto spoke to before his death, told an Inquirer reporter, "Mayor Fox has no control over his officers here. They have always been in the habit of disturbing the peace, as far as we are concerned. We consider them as ignorant and low-lived a set of men as ever trod the soil. All the trouble at 6th and Lombard was caused by the police. Fifty of them interfered with the electors at the polls in the morning. . . . We have been subjected to outrages of all kinds at their hands."

Democratic Mayor Daniel Fox, who was not running for re-election, did go to 6th and Lombard and temporarily calmed the situation. But when he left, the battle was renewed. A steady stream of injured people made their way to Pennsylvania Hospital. Blacks took to the roofs and showered bricks on the heads of white rioters.

The Philadelphia Inquirer wrote: "The scene beggars description. The policemen in their efforts to make arrests fell out of line and became mixed up with the populace, while whites and blacks were jammed together pell-mell and a free fight raged fiercely for a square [a block]. The housetops were crowded, and from many of those on St. Mary's Street brickbats came crashing down on the heads of the multitudes. In the street, paving stones and brickbats were flying in all directions. Every few moments there would be the report of a pistol, a shout or a yell. . . . Murders were perpetrated and people were wounded by the dozens. . . . To all intents it was a grand free fight rather than a riot."

Levi Bolden, a black man, was shot on Lombard Street. He died three weeks later in the hospital. Later that afternoon another black was killed in a particularly vicious manner. A pair of goons followed Isaac Chase down a narrow alley toward his house. He was shot at and slain when one of the pair split his skull with a hatchet. The killers were identified as Reddy Dever and Frank Kelly. In a couple of hours—after the big melee had subsided a bit—the same pair of youthful goons would encounter Catto on South Street.

At the Institute for Colored Youth, which still stands near 10th and Bainbridge but is now a condominium, Catto dismissed the students early. He apparently visited the mayor to appeal for help in ending the violence. He stopped by his National Guard Armory because his unit was on alert. On Chestnut Street, he endured a confrontation with some nasty whites and was threatened with a gun. This spurred Catto to purchase a cheap pistol from a pawnshop. But he did not buy ammunition.

He stopped to see White, mentioned the pistol, and said he had ammunition at home, where he was headed. Perhaps he wanted a loaded gun in his pocket before attempting to vote.

He was steps away from his rooming house when his path crossed those of Reddy Dever and Frank Kelly. There were plenty of people—black and white—on the street. A policeman saw part of the incident. Those on a passing streetcar got a bird's-eye view.

Catto walked past the two men. Some words might have been exchanged. Kelly, his head wrapped in a white bandage, turned, pulled a gun and approached Catto. A black woman screamed a warning. Catto turned and faced Kelly. Two shots were fired. Catto dashed into the street attempting to hide behind the stopped streetcar. Kelly followed and fired at least two more shots into Catto. The coroner found four pistol-ball wounds in the body. One penetrated the heart. (William Minton, a friend and a popular black caterer, was given one of the bullets as a memento.)

Kelly took off, turned onto 9th Street and ducked into a tavern at 9th and Bainbridge. In pursuit were a handful of citizens and a couple of cops. One of the pursuers would later testify that he nabbed Kelly inside the bar and turned him over to two cops. But the police would deny the allegation, claiming the fugitive escaped through the rear door of the taproom. At any rate, Frank Kelly and Reddy Dever disappeared from the city, probably with the full connivance of Squire McMullin. It took another six years before Kelly was located and arrested in Chicago.

It is illuminating to read how the partisan newspapers of the day reported the riots and the death of Catto. The staunchly Republican Bulletin wrote glowingly of Catto's background and character and left no doubt who was responsible for the murder. "He was a good citizen, a pure and honest man, a ripe scholar and a consistent friend of the oppressed negroes. He was worth more to the community and to the world than a million of such men as the Democratic politicians who provoked the riots of yesterday."

The Democratic Philadelphia Ledger begins its report by detailing the difficulties police had in containing rioting blacks and providing names and details of the whites hurt and wounded. It also describes "a gang of drunken colored men congregating about that locality insulting every respectable woman that passed along and spitting at Mrs. McNichol three different times while she was standing on the doorstep, and firing four or five shots at four white men who were walking quietly along and talking to each other." In tones of righteous horror, the Ledger charged that the ax murder of poor Isaac Chase was perpetrated by the same crowd of drunken blacks after the victim told them he had just voted Democratic.

Near the end of the Ledger story we learn that Catto, "a well-known colored man," got into an argument on the street with an unknown white man. "After an animated discussion, Catto drew his revolver, and while some assert that he discharged one barrel, others deny it, but all agree that his opponent drew his revolver and discharged two shots both of which took effect in the heart of Catto." An interesting fact near the bottom of the Ledger story informs us that: "Frank Kelly, a young man, was taken to the hospital with a slight gunshot wound."

The unabashedly racist Philadelphia Age blamed everything on "colored Radical thugs." This newspaper repeats the lie that Chase was killed by his own people for voting Democratic. "His murder was cold-blooded and foul, and his death was the commencement of a determined and premeditated Radical riot."

Catto's funeral was one of the largest in city history. "Thousands gathered about the City Armory at Broad and Race Streets anxious to view the remains of the late Octavius V. Catto . . . in an hour or two the crowd became so dense that a large force of police was required to keep the various avenues open for travel," reported the Philadelphia Press.

A huge entourage accompanied the casket down Broad Street lined "as far as the eye could see by one dense mass of moving, swaying human beings who despite the rain maintained their positions."

The marchers included numerous military units; city officials; "a delegation of prominent colored men from Washington"; various black clubs and organizations, including the Pythian Baseball Club and the tearful students and faculty of the Institute for Colored Youth. A band and an honor firing squad of 20 soldiers did their parts as Catto's casket was lowered into the ground in the now defunct Lebanon Cemetery in South Philadelphia. "Nothing occurred during the entire day to mar the funeral ceremonies, notwithstanding the immense throng present," the Press reported.

Heavy rewards were offered for the arrests of Dever and Kelly. In 1877, Philadelphia police went to Chicago and brought Frank Kelly back for trial. In an era when it was normal to complete a murder trial, from jury selection to verdict, in a single day, the Kelly trial was a marathon, stretching 10 full days.

The two sides called about 35 witnesses. The prosecution called a dozen witnesses, black and white, who either fingered Kelly as the gunman or said it could have been him, but they were not sure. Others testified to seeing the slightly built Kelly in the thick of the earlier fighting. Some witnesses saw him firing at blacks. "He ran a colored man up 8th Street and fired three shots at him," testified one black woman.

John A. Fawcett, a black teen-ager, said Kelly led the group of whites that chased him down South Street. He jumped into an open cellar but not before Kelly had fired four shots, hitting him once in the hip. He kept the bullet on his key chain as a souvenir. Only one witness, a policeman, said Catto had drawn his pistol.

The defense produced eyewitnesses who saw a man with a bandaged head shoot Catto, but swore Kelly was not that man. McMullen testified that he knew several men who had bandaged heads that day. Alibi witness Patrick Smith said that at the time of the Catto shooting, Kelly and Dever were both drunk and sitting on a step on 8th Street. Smith said he went to investigate the commotion created by Catto's murder. When he returned, the pair was sitting on the same steps.

For unexplained reasons, two prosecutors and two defense attorneys gave closing arguments that took a total of 10 hours. Not surprisingly, an all-white, all-male jury returned with a verdict of "Not guilty."

Kelly was also tried for the ax murder of Isaac Chase and was again acquitted with the aid of witness McMullen. Next Reddy Dever returned to the city and was put on trial for Chase's murder. He, too, was acquitted. McMullen's biographer, Harry Silcox, found a note dashed off by the Squire to a political buddy stating, "All quiet here. I have had a hard week's work getting Dever acquitted."

The shameful violence of 1871 gave the Democrats a black eye and provided Republicans with an issue they exploited for a decade.

In his later years, McMullen became something of a beloved public figure, known more for his charitable nature, storytelling and political wisdom than his old, rowdy, two-fisted ways. He died in 1901 at age 77.

The Quaker board of directors at the Institute for Colored Youth gradually shifted the emphasis from academics to vocational skills and finally moved the school to Chester County where it became a farm school that evolved into Cheyney University.

A school at 20th and Lombard was named in Catto's honor in 1878. When it closed in 1913, a new school in West Philadelphia became the Catto School, but it closed in 1989. The black martyr is nearly forgotten.

Millions of copies of this sketch of little Charley Ross
were distributed across America and overseas.

CHAPTER 3

America's Lost Boy
Charley Ross

Without doubt, the biggest criminal case in Philadelphia history, in terms of intense nationwide interest, was the kidnapping for ransom of an adorable, flaxen-haired, four-year-old boy in the summer of 1874.

In every aspect, the abduction of "Little Charley Ross" rivaled the sensation of the Lindbergh Baby kidnapping some 50 years later. An entire nation seemed to share the anguish and heartache of one unfortunate family. It was a story—full of emotion, mystery, pathos—that would dominate the news for many months and reappear with regularity over many decades.

All the shock and fascination was evoked, in great measure, because it had never happened before in America. Holding a child for ransom was associated only with Sicily and other "backward" areas of the Mediterranean. It was a crime totally alien to America.

For decades the name *Charley Ross* would be invoked constantly by parents from Oregon to Maryland warning their children, "Never take candy from a stranger. Remember what happened to little Charley Ross; Never go with a stranger. Remember little Charley Ross."

The most compelling criminal drama in Philadelphia annals started with a vague feeling of concern on the part of merchant Christian K. Ross when he returned to his Germantown home from his Market Street dry goods store on the evening of July 1. Ross' youngest boys, Walter, 6, and Charles, 4, weren't there to greet his arrival.

There were seven children in the family. Ross' wife, Sarah, in poor health, was resting in Atlantic City with her eldest daughter. Two older boys were in Middletown, Pa., with their paternal grandmother. The two small boys and two daughters were at home, cared for by nursemaids. There were also a cook and a gardener in the household.

The nannies said the boys had been given baths. They then went to play in front of the house. Ross, the girls and nannies went looking for the boys. The family lived in a large stone Victorian house on Washington Lane, west of Main Street, which is now called Germantown Avenue. It was set back 50 feet from the street, shielded with a lot of trees and shrubbery.

A neighbor told Ross she had heard Walter and Charley talking to two strange men. And she thought she saw the boys pass by her house in a wagon. Night was falling. Ross was suddenly filled with alarm. He started toward Germantown Avenue and the neighborhood police station. Suddenly, a wave of relief came over the worried father as he saw a stranger walking toward him holding Walter's hand. That relief was short-lived.

The man was a Good Samaritan who had found Walter alone and crying on a sidewalk at Palmer and Richmond streets in Kensington—eight miles from the Ross home. "Where is Charley?" asked the father. "He's in the wagon," answered the boy.

The story emerged. Two men with a horse and buggy had stopped to talk with the kids and offer candy on a couple of occasions earlier in the week. That evening the same pair appeared on Washington Lane again. The two again engaged the boys in conversation. Independence Day was approaching, and the boys were excitedly anticipating their father's setting off rockets and firecrackers.

The men offered to take Walter and Charley to a store to buy firecrackers. The boys were lifted into the buggy, and off they went. Walter was frightened as they left the neighborhood. The men calmed him, saying they were going to "Aunt Susie's" store where he could get a pocketful of firecrackers for five cents.

The buggy took a long, indirect route. The pair chatted with the boys who were seated in a way that hid them from view by people along the route. Finally, they reached Aunt Susie's store. Walter was given a quarter and told to buy whatever he wanted. When the six-year-old emerged from the shop, the buggy and Charley were gone.

Ross, the Good Samaritan and Walter rushed down to Kensington in search of Charley or the buggy or any witnesses. No luck. They went to central police headquarters and reported the boy lost. All police stations in the city were queried. Did they have a lost boy of four with curly blond hair? The response was negative. Ross returned home after midnight to spend the first of many sleepless nights.

The next day the frightened father met with the chief of detectives and placed an advertisement in the Philadelphia papers giving a description and offering a reward for Charley's return. That evening he met with detectives, the chief of police, the district attorney and Mayor William Stokey. The theory offered by officials was that a couple of drunks had taken the boy; when they sobered up, he would be released.

Walter provided good descriptions of both men, plus descriptions of the unusual buggy and the bay horse, which had distinctive markings. He had also paid attention to the route taken. With all this information, police were sure they would soon find the boy. But detectives also subjected the anxious father to a long interrogation about his personal life.

The next day, a band of Gypsies camped in West Philadelphia were rounded up and questioned. For the next year no band of Gypsies or itinerant travelers on the East Coast with a child in their group would escape detention and interrogation. Posters giving an account of the abduction were prepared by police.

On July 4th, a weary Christian Ross sat in the police station with his fingers crossed. Suddenly the merchant's brother, Joseph Ross, rushed in waving a letter. The mysterious disappearance was explained and a horrible new phase of the Charley Ross Story began. The letter was the first of 26 missives the kidnappers would mail to Ross from July 3 to early November.

A weird handwriting, strange spelling and near-lack of punctuation characterize all the letters. The first was relatively short. The others would ramble on for many pages. In part, the first missive said:

"Ros—be not uneasy you son charly bruster be al writ we is got him and no power on earth can deliver out of our hands—You will hav two pay us befor you git him from us—an pay a big cent. . . . if any approch is maid to his hidin place that is the signil for his instant anihilation . . . you money can fetch him out alive an no other existin powers—dont deceve yuself an think the detectives can git him from us for that is one imposebel—you here from us in a few days."

When the little boy was asked his name, he would always respond with the full "Charles Brewster Ross." The use of "charly bruster" was strong proof that the writer really had the Ross boy.

It was an extraordinary event. True, on rare occasions children had been snatched by deranged persons. There were cases of a very poor child being abducted and trained to beg on the streets. But this was the first time a child of a wealthy family was kidnapped for ransom.

From that first letter to the last, police, the mayor, newspapers and a committee of prominent citizens—which soon formed to aid and advise the family—were unanimous and adamant on one point: No ransom must be paid. They reasoned that no child in America would be safe if the kidnappers succeeded. The strategy that emerged was to play a chess game with the villains. String them along. Play for time. Eventually the culprits would be caught because the entire nation was looking for little Charley Ross.

It was a huge story. Major newspapers from other cities sent reporters to cover the unfolding drama in Philadelphia. The only thing police held back from the press was the texts of the letters.

Others in Germantown had glimpsed the kidnappers because they had been seen in the neighborhood several times that week. One man was young, perhaps in his late 20s. The other was about 50. Both had chin whiskers. The older man wore goggles, and Walter said he had "a monkey nose." This was an important clue that police failed to exploit. The older kidnapper did, indeed, have a strangely deformed nose that might have rung bells with certain detectives in New York City.

All roads in and out of the city, the waterfront and all train stations were put under police surveillance. Known criminal hangouts were raided. And before July was over, frustrated police had launched an unprecedented house-by-house search of every building in the city. More than 100,000 buildings of every sort were searched over several weeks.

Scores of people visited the Ross house to offer advice and sympathy. Letters arrived from across the nation and Europe with unsolicited advice, sympathy and prayers. And soon little Charley Ross was "found" in scores of places.

Christian Ross, his brother or brothers-in-law would take countless trips—sometimes to the Deep South or the Midwest—to look at boys who local police felt certain was the missing child.

The events of July 30 provide an example of the many false hopes. It was important for another reason, too. That morning the Philadelphia Times blazed across its front page the joyous news that Charley had been found. The news spread and the excitement in Philadelphia was intense. The Pottsville police telegrammed to report that a four-year-old boy—a boy who conformed in every respect to Charley Ross—had been found in a Gypsy camp near Hamburg, Pa. The citizens of that town had surrounded the Gypsy camp enmasse until police arrived to liberate Charley.

The Philadelphia police chief, several officers and Ross' brother-in-law were provided a special train by the Reading Railroad for the 75-mile-trip. The entire line was cleared of traffic. Crowds waited along the line and next to newspaper offices for final confirmation. By late afternoon, all the joy and hopes were dashed. It wasn't Charley. In fact, the child was much too young and bore a strong resemblance to the frightened, dark-skinned woman who protested that she was the boy's mother.

Later that day Ross received another letter—the 11th—from the kidnappers. Although they mailed letters from various points, Ross had been instructed to communicate through the personal ads in certain newspapers. He knew by now they wanted $20,000. Despite his fears, he had followed police instructions and had been stalling. Now they had reached the point of making a deal or risking a break in communications.

The July 30th letter gave Ross exact instructions on how to deliver the money. And if the money was good and unmarked, Charley would be released in hours. The father was instructed to take a certain train leaving Philadelphia at midnight for New York City, then switch to another train from New York to Albany. He was to stand on the outside platform of the last car in both trains. The letter said, "...yu may not go one mile befor our agent meets yu and yet yu may go 250 before he intercepts yu."

The kidnappers' "agent" would be standing by the tracks, signaling with a torch in one hand and a flag in the other. As soon as the father spotted the signal, he must toss a valise with the money onto the tracks. If the agent was arrested, it would mean instant death for the child.

The police decided that Ross must make the trip. But instead of money, the valise would contain a letter to the kidnappers. It demanded more proof that they actually had Charley plus other delaying arguments. The father was accompanied by a plainclothes detective and his brother-in-law. It was an excruciating ordeal, emotionally and physically. Ross was near collapse by the time the second train reached Albany. But there had been no signal.

The next day Letter Twelve arrived, and it became clear that the kidnappers read the newspaper, too. They believed the father had gone on the wild-goose chase to Pottsville instead of waiting for instructions. That is why they hadn't followed through.

Christian Ross and his wife were under unbearable pressure. Police and the advisory committee were firm: They must not give in to the kidnappers' demand for money for the sake of every other parent. The unspoken message was: You must sacrifice your child for the sake of all others. Of course, the police argued that Charley would never be murdered because he would be of no value dead.

But the author of the ransom letters was a master psychologist, playing on the parents' guilt and fears with virtuoso skill. Each letter accurately and sarcastically pointed out that the police investigation had thus far produced nothing. Turn to the detectives after the child is safely home, wrote the kidnapper. But now, there was only one party in the universe who could rescue little Charley—and that was his father. Was money more important than the life of his son? And if Charley died "unredeemed" by his parents that was "alright," too, because it would provide a lesson that would insure quick payment from the next victim.

The letters were bold, brimming with self-confidence, threats of death and the solemn promise of a square-deal for the father if he dealt honestly with them. The writer said Charley was kept by others. From time to time, the writer offered information about Charley's health and things the boy said, both to prove they really had Charley and to ratchet up the mental torture of the distressed parents.

And tortured they were. By early fall, Christian Ross suffered a nervous collapse and was bedridden for several weeks before he was again able to return to the daily effort of bringing his son home. The press didn't help. In the beginning, newspapers leveled unending criticism at Philadelphia police and officials for their total lack of success in either finding Charlie or identifying the criminals.

Worse, for a time, the press was filled with poisonous innuendo aimed at the Ross family. It was alleged that Ross' business was not doing well, and this was true. Were there family secrets? Was Charley really the child of Mrs. Ross?

Then, The Reading Eagle published a story under the headline "Ross Case All Humbug" which set new lows in malicious, libelous journalism. The article said Ross was a bigamist, with a second wife who was the real mother of Walter and Charley. It stated that Ross was bankrupt. The other wife had taken Charley. And the kidnap letters were all forgeries written by Ross himself. The tortured father had to answer this attack. A libel suit resulted in a $1,000 judgment and The Eagle was blasted by the court for gross abuse of the press.

The committee to aid the Ross family raised a $20,000 reward for information leading to the arrest and conviction of the kidnappers. More money was raised and the famous Pinkerton National Detective Agency—the closest thing at the time to an FBI—was hired. The Secret Service pledged its help in the efforts to find Charley.

Seven million copies of a circular containing Charley's picture and other data were sent to every sheriff in the nation, every railroad office and steamship line. Some went overseas. The sketch of Charley was made by an artist using a baby photo and descriptions of the boy as he looked at the time of the kidnapping.

In August there was a major breakthrough that was withheld from the public. The superintendent of New York City Police, George Washington Walling, telegrammed Philadelphia police: "Send detective here with original letters of kidnappers of Ross child; think I have information."

The promising information came from a boat builder and ex-thief, Gil Mosher. Mosher believed his own brother, William "Bill" Mosher, and Bill's friend Joseph Douglas were the kidnappers. Bill Mosher and Douglas had met in Sing-Sing Prison. Mosher fit the description of the older kidnapper and Douglas matched the younger man.

More important, Gil Mosher claimed that a few months prior to the Ross kidnapping, his brother had invited him to join a plot to kidnap one of the grandchildren of millionaire Cornelius Vanderbilt. They would hold the Vanderbilt child in a boat and demand $50,000 ransom. Gil felt it was too risky and rejected the idea. He gave the police commissioner aliases used by his brother and Douglas, but said he hadn't seen the pair in a long time.

Although he could provide no samples of his brother's handwriting, Gil Mosher described Bill's idiosyncratic writing style. When the Philadelphia detective arrived with the letters, they matched Mosher's description exactly.

Bill Mosher was about 50, the husband of a young woman and the father of several children. He was a skilled burglar who knew every foot of New York's rivers and bays and Long Island Sound. His normal modus operandi was to rob houses along the shore and escape by boat.

The effort now was to find Mosher and Douglas. Commissioner Walling turned to Bill Mosher's brother-in-law, William Westervelt, a former city policeman, dismissed for allegedly protecting an illegal lottery. He maintained his innocence and was fighting to get his job back. Westervelt's wife and Bill Mosher's wife were sisters.

There was a remarkable series of 50 meetings over several months between Walling and Westervelt. Although Westervelt professed to know nothing of the kidnapping and didn't think Mosher was capable of such a dastardly crime, he knew a lot about the comings and goings of the two suspects. It came out slowly, piecemeal.

Eventually, Westervelt revealed that Mosher, his wife and kids had been living in Philadelphia at the time of the kidnapping. In fact, Westervelt had visited the family there and told Walling their old address on Monroe Street and the location of the stable where Mosher kept his horse.

Mosher had disappeared about the time of the kidnapping, said Westervelt. In August he helped his sister-in-law move back to New York. She and the kids stayed in his apartment awhile. And Mosher and Douglas arrived one evening for an unexpected visit. Since then he had "accidentally" bumped into both men on the streets of New York; they had a couple beers together. Commissioner Walling was never quite certain if Westervelt was a party to the kidnapping or sincerely trying to help.

In the meantime, the correspondence between kidnapper and Ross family continued. By November the broken family decided to ignore the police and pay the ransom. Using a code name, the Ross family advertised that on November 18, they would be at the Fifth Avenue Hotel in New York City with the unmarked $20,000. Unknown to the family, police watched the hotel. No contact was made. It was the last attempt to ransom Charley. There were no more letters from the kidnappers.

One month later came the most dramatic and unexpected twist in the national drama.

December 13, 1874 was truly "a dark and stormy night" at Bay Ridge, Long Island. On that cold, rainy night, two burglars broke into a large, vacant summerhouse owned by a judge. The judge's brother, Holmes Van Brunt, lived in a house about 200 yards distant. A burglar alarm had been rigged from the mansion to Van Brunt's house.

The alarm sounded and Van Brunt sent his son to investigate. He returned quickly to report seeing a faint light flickering in the upper windows. Van Brunt, his son, a gardener and a hired-hand armed themselves with revolvers and shotguns and crept up to the mansion. They could make out two men moving about inside.

When the pair emerged, Van Brunt ordered them to halt. In response, the burglars opened fire with pistols. The four armed men shot back. When the smoke cleared both burglars lay on the ground. None of the Bay Ridge men were hurt.

One burglar was dead. The other was badly wounded. He identified himself as Joseph Douglas and his companion as Bill Mosher. He had a confession to make to the crowd of villagers which soon gathered. "It's no use lying now," he said. "Mosher and I stole Charley Ross from Germantown."

When the amazed villagers asked why they stole the boy, Douglas answered simply, "To make money." Asked where the Ross boy was, Douglas replied, "Mosher knows all about the child. Ask him." Assured that Mosher was dead and pressed for more information, Douglas said he didn't know but added, "The child will be returned home safe and sound in a few days." A few minutes later, Douglas was dead. At that point, only the police officials in New York and Philadelphia knew that the pair was being sought.

The story was Page One. Little Walter Ross was brought to the New York City morgue and positively identified the dead men as the same pair that took Charley and himself for the buggy ride six months earlier. And Mosher did have a deformed nose—like a monkey.

Excited Philadelphians swarmed into the streets. They congregated near newspaper offices where new details were put up on display boards. Most people believed that Charley Ross would soon appear—dropped off on some city street or at a church with a note pinned to his jacket. Days passed. Weeks passed. Decades past.

Charley Ross was never found. Christian Ross and his wife spent the rest of their lives searching for their lost boy.

But there was another dramatic chapter to come when Westervelt was brought to Philadelphia and charged with being one of the kidnappers. His trial in the summer of 1875 generated nearly as much interest as the

Lindbergh trial five decades later. A mountain of circumstantial evidence was introduced which seemed to show that Westervelt had played the role of double agent. He seemed to be aiding police but was in close communication with the kidnappers, providing them information on the cops' movements.

A female witness claimed she saw Westervelt on a Brooklyn trolley with Charley a few days after the kidnapping. A friend testified Westervelt used the term "us" when talking about the kidnappers.

But the defendant emphatically denied everything. The last question his lawyer asked was whether Westervelt could provide any information on the fate of little Charley Ross. "No sir," he answered. "I wished to God I could."

The 15-day trial was long by 19th-century standards and left all the basic questions unanswered. In his charge, the judge said the kidnapping "has been widely regarded as the worst crime of the century." The jury acquitted Westervelt of charges connected to the abduction, but convicted him of extortion and conspiracy. He spent six years at Eastern State Penitentiary.

Christian Ross wrote a best-selling book on the kidnapping, primarily to raise funds to continue his search. He often said that knowing for sure that Charley was dead would at least bring closure to the family's misery. "A fixed calamity abates with time," he wrote. "The sorrow of suspense grows intenser."

Police and the public kept "finding" Charley. Before his death in 1897, Ross estimated that 500 to 600 potential Charleys had been brought to his attention, some found as far away as Germany. Scores of orphan boys or imaginative runaways arrived in Philadelphia claiming they were Charley. Letters poured into the Ross home for decades. Mostly they came from crackpots, but there were also extortion attempts—money for information. Christian Ross died in 1897. His wife kept up the search until her death in 1912.

There was a spate of newspaper and magazine stories in 1924 to mark the 50th anniversary of the kidnapping. Stockbroker Walter Ross was interviewed and said crank letters were still received and middle-aged men were still claiming to be Charley. The Ross house was sold to a nearby church, which demolished the once handsome mansion in 1926.

In 1939, a man in his late 60s from Arizona went to court, suing for the right to use his real name, *Charles Brewster Ross.* He had a most adventurous tale to tell of his kidnapping and subsequent life. Since no one contested the suit, the Arizona court declared the man to be Charley Ross. Old Charley Ross then rushed off to Hollywood to peddle his story to the movie studios—without success.

Herman Mudgett, known to the world as H.H. Holmes,
and his Chicago "Murder Castle."

CHAPTER 4

The Diabolical Mr. Mudgett
H.H. Holmes

Never before had the city known such an intriguing detective story as the startling saga which began unfolding in late 1894. Never before had there been such a diabolically evil criminal at the center of such a tangled and incredible plot.

Never before had Americans been exposed to such a twisted, murderous, cunning and duplicitous personality as that of Herman W. Mudgett aka H.H. Holmes. Neither Poe nor Hitchcock could have improved on the real-life master of Chicago's "Murder Castle," where between 27 and 200 young women met a murderous end. Holmes stands apart from our modern, run-of-the-mill, maniac serial killer because he was also a bold and highly-imaginative, full-time swindler and confidence man.

This fantastic tale, which ended on the gallows at Moyamensing Prison in South Philadelphia, began to unfold in late August 1894 when a sign appeared in the window of 1316 Callowhill Street reading: "B.F. Perry Patents Bought and Sold." At that time, there were brick rowhouses on one side of Callowhill and an abandoned railroad yard on the other. The new business bought and marketed inventions.

Soon after the sign went up, carpenter Eugene Smith stopped to talk to the patent man about a tool he had invented. The tall, lanky Perry asked to see a model and also hired the carpenter to return the next day to build a store counter. While he was working on the counter, a man entered Perry's place. The stranger, later identified by Smith as H.H. Holmes, was motioned upstairs where the two spoke alone.

On September 3, Smith stopped by the office to check Perry's progress in selling his invention. The door was unlocked but no one was there. Smith hung around for a while, but Perry never showed. The next morning Smith returned to find the door still unlocked and there was still no Perry. The carpenter shouted and climbed the steps to the second floor where he made a gruesome discovery.

A corpse was stretched out on the floor of the rear room. The cadaver's face was burned beyond recognition and parts of the upper body were charred. Smith rushed out and returned with police. It seemed as if the man had died in an explosion. Next to the body was a large broken bottle, a burned match and a pipe filled with tobacco that was slightly charred.

By convenient chance the Callowhill Street house was directly behind the city morgue. An autopsy showed that the man had died quickly, either from the flames or the inhalation of chloroform, because there was a strong odor of chloroform in the lungs of the corpse.

The body was kept in the morgue for 10 days, and when no friend or family came to claim the corpse, it was buried in the city's potter's field. Then a letter arrived at the Fidelity Mutual Life Insurance Company in Philadelphia from Jeptha D. Howe, a lawyer from St. Louis. Howe's missive stated that he was sure a man who died in an explosion under the name Perry was really Benjamin F. Pitezel, who was insured by the company for $10,000. Howe said he represented the widow and the couple's five children. He arranged to come East with a daughter of Pitezel—the widow was ill— to identify the body and collect the insurance money. Still another letter arrived from Indianapolis. The writer, H.H. Holmes, declared he had known Pitezel for many years. He was coming east on business and would gladly aid in identifying the mysterious corpse.

Holmes and lawyer Howe, with 14-year-old Alice Pitezel, arrived at the insurance office on the same day. Apparently the two men didn't know each other and were introduced. Alice did know her father's friend Holmes. Holmes ticked off several distinguishing characteristics of Pitezel—oddly spaced teeth, a mole on the back of his neck, a scar on one leg, a twisted fingernail.

The rotting remains were dug up; by this time the stench was horrendous. The helpful Holmes put on rubber gloves and found the mole, pointed out the scar and other marks and concluded it was, indeed, the body of Pitezel. A covering was put over the corpse's face with a slit so only the teeth could be seen. Alice was brought into the room. She agreed; it was her father. The insurance officials were convinced that the dead man was Pitezel and presented Howe with a $10,000 check for the widow.

The story might have ended there. But several weeks later, the St. Louis police commissioner received a letter from an inmate in the local jail. The writer was Marion Hedgepath, a notorious train robber. Hedgepath wrote that a former cellmate, an accused swindler, named H.M. Howard, had let him in on an insurance-fraud scheme. Howard planned to insure an associate named Pitezel. Then he would pass off a morgue cadaver as Pitezel and collect the cash. The crafty Howard boasted that he had pulled the same sort of fraud in the past with success. He asked Hedgepath to recommend a lawyer who would assist in the plot. The inmate recommended his own lawyer's brother, Jeptha D. Howe. For his help, swindler Howard promised to pay Hedgepath $500. Of course, the train robber never saw a penny. The police commissioner notified the insurance company, which sent its top detective, W.E. Gary, to look into the matter. Over the next year, the criminal career of Mudgett/Holmes/Howard would amaze and shock the nation.

Mudgett hailed from the small town of Gilmanton, N.H. He had been a bright student. At 18 he married a local girl, Clara A. Lovering, and then fathered two children. Apparently Clara and the kids stayed with her parents while Herman went to college in Vermont and afterward attended medical school at the University of Michigan in Ann Arbor.

According to one account, Mudgett was expelled from medical school when he was caught trying to sneak a body out of the anatomy lab. But he didn't return home: He abandoned his wife and kids, who heard nothing from him for the next 10 years. He appeared in Chicago as Harry H. Holmes about 1885 and soon graduated to bigamy by marrying the daughter of a well-to-do family in suburban Wilmette and fathering another three kids.

A lot has been written about Holmes, but his story is rife with myth and guesswork. Unfortunately, it is difficult to separate fact from fiction because the journalism of the day was none too accurate. And there was no point in Chicago police' doing a thorough investigation because the arch-villain was soon swinging from a gallows in Philadelphia.

In Chicago, Holmes dabbled in real estate fraud. He operated drugstores and sold phony nostrums, passing off bottles of tap water as surefire cures for every ailment. One writer said the clever bunko artist built a washing machine-size contraption in his basement. Holmes said the complex Rube Goldberg maze of pipes, pulleys and wires could turn water into gas for lighting. After a successful demonstration, Holmes sold the wonderful device to a Canadian for $2,000. It was difficult to discern, but one pipe tapped into a gas company main.

But Holmes' greatest skill was seducing women and bilking them out of their property or cash. The man was not only handsome, he was charming, glib and slick as a cat's whisker.

In 1892 we find Holmes working in a drugstore owned by a widow and somehow ending up as owner of the property at 63rd and Wallace in the Englewood area of Chicago. Then he purchased an empty lot on the other side of the street where he built a large, complex structure that became infamous as "H.H. Holmes' Murder Castle."

Ostensibly, he was building a hotel to take advantage of visitors who would soon be streaming into Chicago during the 1893 Columbian

Exposition Fair. It was a rambling, ugly, three-story structure with store-fronts on the ground floor. Holmes started hiring young women who rented rooms on the third floor. Some accounts say he started a stenography business; others say he simply kept the girls busy with useless paperwork.

One thing is certain: Holmes had set up a crazy-quilt complex of secret rooms on the second floor and basement of his odd property. It was a true chamber of horrors that could serve as the set of a Hollywood chiller. There were staircases that led nowhere, hinged walls, false partitions and bricked-in gas chambers. The Chicago newspapers described "a five-door room," "a closed room with a dummy elevator," "the blind room," and "the secret chamber." Most ominous was a room in the center of the house reached through a trapdoor in the bathroom. It had a chute going straight to the basement. And in the basement were found dissecting tables, a crematory and two lime pits. Doors to all the secret rooms were wired to an alarm system.

No one knows how many women perished in the "Castle" nor exactly what motivated Holmes' homicidal hobby. Before his execution, he confessed to 27 slayings. An imaginative police official estimated that the number of victims might be as high as 200. But 20 to 30 murders during a two-year period seems the most honest estimate.

Although some human bones were found in the basement, Holmes had done a stellar job eliminating the bodies. In fact, he often sold skeletons to medical schools. It is believed that most of the Castle killings involved bilking the women out of their money. But the creation of such a diabolical murder factory leaves little doubt that the man was also a homicidal psychopath.

Not only did Holmes maintain his marriage in Wilmette, but he, moreover, kept another woman at the Castle. People in the neighborhood assumed that Mrs. Julia Conner was Holmes' wife. And police believe Conner and her child were the swindler's first murder victims.

The next mistress of the Castle was young Minnie Williams from Texas who had inherited a good deal of property in Fort Worth. She was joined by her younger sister, Anna. There is a belief that Minnie was an accomplice in some of Holmes' scams. At any rate, both sisters disappeared forever and were probably dispatched by Holmes.

He was a busy little beaver in the months prior to the Philadelphia caper because he was low on cash. He rarely paid bills and a lot of creditors were on his back. Not only was he involved with Minnie Williams, but in January 1894 he married for a third time—to pretty young Georgianna Yoke who would eventually testify at his trial.

The myth and speculation surrounding this world-class criminal end when Holmes was arrested for the Philadelphia insurance case. Philadelphia Detective Frank P. Geyer was a skilled sleuth and an equally excellent writer. In 1896 Geyer wrote *The Holmes-Pitezel Case: A History of the Greatest Crime of the Century.* It details the investigation that brought Holmes to the gallows and contains verbatim statements Holmes made to police. The transcript of his trial in Philadelphia was also published in book form.

Geyer and the insurance company detectives caught up with Holmes in Boston on November 17th, 1894—a little more than two months after the body was found on Callowhill Street. He cooperated in bringing Mrs. Pitezel to Boston, where she, too, was arrested.

Helpful and loquacious, Holmes soon gave a statement admitting the insurance fraud. Anyone reading his statement soon finds that the man was an actor and a master of the art of double-talk. Detective Geyer writes, "Holmes is greatly given to lying with a sort of florid ornamentation, and all the stories are decorated with flamboyant draperies by him to strengthen the plausibility of his statements. Talking, he has the appearance of candor, becomes pathetic at times when pathos will seem best to him, utters his words with a quaver in the voice often accompanied by a moistened eye, then turning quickly with a determined and forceful method of speech, as if indignation or resolution had sprung out of tender memories that had touched his heart."

Cutting through the blizzard of verbiage, the suspect said the body was shipped in a trunk to Philadelphia from New York by a doctor, whom he refused to name. Pitezel using Holmes' instruction disfigured the face. Now, Pitezel was on the lam with three of his children and was probably in South America or somewhere in the Deep South. He said that for several weeks before his capture, he and Mrs. Pitezel had been hopscotching around the nation and Canada in order to rendezvous with Pitezel and reunite the family. Holmes said he had talked to Pitezel in Detroit but before the family could be reunited, Pitezel was off to Toronto.

The detectives found Mrs. Pitezel to be a distraught and thoroughly confused woman who hadn't seen her husband since July 9. At first she believed he was dead. Then Holmes let her in on the insurance scam and assured her he was alive. After identifying the body in Philadelphia, Holmes told her that he took young Alice to Indianapolis and left her in the good care of a certain Miss Williams. Then he took her son Howard, 12, and a daughter, Nellie, to Miss Williams. This would make travel easier, Holmes explained.

Next Holmes directed Carrie Pitezel and her remaining two children, Jeanette, 16 (known as Dessie), and one-year-old Wharton, to travel to

Detroit where she would be reunited with her husband and the three other children. It hadn't worked out, explained Mrs. Pietzel. The next stop was Toronto. She said next they traveled to Prescott, Canada. Then they crossed the border to Ogdensburg, N.Y. Finally, Holmes rented a house for her and the two children in Burlington, Vt. Shortly after their arrival, Carrie Pitezel said she caught Holmes down in the basement digging with a shovel.

Boston police had a warrant for Holmes from Fort Worth, where he was wanted for stealing a horse. Surprisingly, he said he preferred facing the insurance-fraud rap in Philadelphia to Texas justice. On the train from Boston, Holmes tried to convince a guard to be hypnotized. When that failed, he offered the man $500 "for purposes not stated but quite well understood," wrote Geyer.

In Philadelphia, Holmes was questioned closely and finally dictated a second confession. As detectives suspected, no cadaver had ever been shipped to Pitezel by the mysterious New York doctor. The body found in the Callowhill Street house was really Pitezel. How had he died? Holmes blandly asserted his partner in fraud had committed suicide with chloroform and left a suicide note. Quizzed on the whereabouts of the three missing children, Holmes provided a long, complicated story on their movements. But now, Holmes asserted Miss Williams had the children in London. In fact, helpful Holmes even provided an address on "Vader Street." But there was no such street in London. Investigators felt strongly that Holmes had murdered the children somewhere along the route. "Why should I kill the children?" Holmes protested tearfully.

Eight months after the children were last seen, Geyer embarked on a cross-country odyssey to locate the missing kids, dead or alive. His search was aided by letters the children had written to their mother and grandparents. They had been given to Holmes, but he had never posted them; and they were found in his luggage. The 20-year police veteran carried photographs of Holmes and the children and was aided by keen public interest spawned by the sensational news emerging from the Chicago "Castle."

The top police officials in each city aided Geyer in his quest. His first stop was Cincinnati. He checked hotels around the train station and soon hit upon a registration under one of Mudgett's many aliases. He also found clerks and cleaning personnel who recognized photos of the children and of their "uncle," H.H. Holmes. The detective was then off to Chicago to check with police there. He would continue on to Detroit and Toronto, all the while immersed in very fascinating and clever investigative work.

Perhaps, Geyer's most astounding discovery was evidence that while Holmes was moving the children from city to city, he was also spending time with the unknowing mother in those same cities. Simultaneously, he was also with his third wife, Georgianna, on the Detroit and Toronto legs. The man was bouncing between the hotel where the children were registered, a second where Mrs. Pitezel and the two kids were staying and a third where Georgianna was ensconced. At one point, poor Carrie Pitezel was 10 minutes from her children in Detroit but never knew it.

Geyer was expecting to find bodies in Detroit when he located a house Holmes rented for a few days but quickly abandoned. The detective found an area in the cellar which had been dug up in the recent past, but unearthed no bodies.

In Toronto, Geyer and local police visited real estate offices with the photos and discovered a pretty little cottage on St. Vincent Street where Holmes had paid a month's rent but disappeared from within days. A neighbor remembered Holmes; he had lent his new neighbor a spade. Geyer and the Toronto detectives borrowed the same shovel. A soft spot in the low-ceilinged cellar was found. "The deeper we dug the more horrible the odor became, and when we reached three feet we discovered what appeared to be the bone of a forearm of a human being," wrote the detective. In a short time, they uncovered the pitiful remains of Alice and Nellie Pitezel. A toy the girls played with was found in the house.

"Toronto went wild with excitement," Geyer wrote. The news spread nationwide. Carrie Pitezel, who had been exonerated in the plot, was rushed to Toronto. Geyer warned her "to prepare for the worst." Only hair (washed by the coroner) of both girls and the teeth of one girl were shown to the mother. "The shrieks of that poor, forlorn creature still ring in my ears," wrote Geyer.

But where was the body of the boy, Howard? Geyer went back to Detroit for another search, but he had a hunch that Howard Pitezel had been separated from his sisters back in Indianapolis and murdered there. Despite newspaper publicity, no good leads turned up in Indiana. Geyer returned to Philadelphia to confer with his bosses and then made a third trip to Indianapolis.

Every real estate office was checked. Geyer's last stop before returning home was to the Indianapolis suburb of Irvington. Bingo! A real estate man recognized Holmes' photo as the man who had rented a house months before. And he had a boy with him. The entire neighborhood watched as the house, yard and a shed were searched by police for clues. When it began turning dark, police called off the search.

But some teen-age boys decided to play detective on their own. They entered the basement which contained a large furnace. One teen stuck his arm into the chimney, dislodging a lot of soot—and some teeth and bone. Geyer and the police rushed back. "At the bottom of the chimney we found quite a large charred mass," he writes. It contained the lungs, liver and other charred internal organs of the missing Pitezel boy.

One of the many extraordinary aspects of Holmes' journeys is his New England sojourn prior to his capture in Boston. He knew police—including the Pinkertons—were on his trail. And he decided after all these years of absence to visit his family. Both his parents and his legal wife and children were in New Hampshire and knew nothing of his whereabouts. Suddenly, he appeared with a most amazing tale. According to long-lost Herman, he had been injured terribly in a train wreck. When he regained consciousness, he was a total amnesiac without a clue to his past. He had fallen in love with a wonderful woman who visited the hospital and read to him, and they had married. Now, suddenly, memories of his family in New Hampshire had returned.

Holmes' trial for the murder of Pitezel kicked off October 28, 1895. His two lawyers demanded more time to prepare their defense; one, Samuel Rotan, would later become Philadelphia district attorney. When the judge refused to delay the trial, the defense lawyers backed out, but returned to the courtroom after Holmes did a stellar job on his own during jury selection. The trial lasted six days. Holmes presented no witnesses and did not take the stand. He often joined in cross-examining state witnesses and did a creditable job as a lawyer.

Rotan gave a lengthy closing. He agreed there was a plan to defraud the insurance company, but insisted Pitezel had committed suicide. The lawyer focused on the medical evidence and asked the jury, "Can you imagine a man being killed in any way which would point more to suicide than this case?"

As Rotan told it, poor Holmes had been shocked to discover his friend's body and a note reading, "Collect the insurance. Look out for the family. I have committed suicide." Holmes decided to do the best he could for Pitezel's family. The insurance company would not pay on a suicide, so he tried to make the death look like an accident. And, argued Rotan, Holmes came to Philadelphia from Boston and cooperated in the firm belief that he had only committed fraud and expected a two-year prison sentence.

Despite the lawyer's best arguments, the jury returned after two hours with a verdict of guilty of murder in the first degree. Appeals citing numerous procedural errors were filed, and quickly dismissed.

At Moyamensing Prison, Holmes converted to Catholicism and wrote an extraordinary confession giving every horrifying detail of 27 murders. One amazing aspect of the confession was Holmes' assertion that he was undergoing a physical transformation. He said he was taking on the appearance of the devil.

He apparently loved the limelight. If he must hang, he wanted to be remembered in history as the world's most fiendish villain. Of course, his appearance was not changing and the confession was a mixture of truth and the imaginative mind of a devoted reader of Edgar Allan Poe. In fact, three or four of his alleged victims turned up alive.

Just before his execution the audacious criminal tried several ploys to delay the hangman, such as writing to Geyer that an accomplice had actually killed the three Pitezel children. Now the noble Holmes wanted to work with the detective to catch the real killer. The man who had just confessed to 27 murders even applied to the governor of Pennsylvania for clemency.

Several thousand people sought permission to watch the hanging inside the prison yard at "Moko," but there was space for only 60 lucky witnesses. Holmes slept soundly the night before his execution and was cool and composed as he stood on the gallows on May 7. Before the trap was sprung, the amazing Mr. Holmes had a statement to make. "I would make no remarks at this time were it not for my feeling that in not speaking I would acquiesce in my execution." He then astounded everyone by declaring he had killed only two unnamed women and was totally innocent of the murder of Pietzel and the three Pietzel children.

Prior to his last day, Holmes had made a last request of Rotan, which the lawyer dutifully carried out. Holmes was rightfully afraid that his body would be dug up, perhaps by a P.T. Barnum-type promoter. In fact, Rotan had been offered $5,000 for the body, and doctors had requested the serial killer's brain for post-mortem study.

His final request was for an extra-large casket with enough room for his body and plenty of cement. In fact, he was entombed in several tons of cement before the casket was lowered into an unmarked grave at Holy Cross Cemetery in Delaware County.

One obvious mystery surrounding the case was the inexplicable cross-country wanderings and the murder of the three Pitezel children. Detective Geyer's theory was that Holmes and Pitezel owned some Texas property jointly but Holmes would gain clear title only if Pitezel's entire family was eliminated. Killing the mother and her five children turned out to be a more complicated and time-consuming task than Holmes had reckoned. He had eliminated the father and three children, but was caught before he could complete the job.

In the middle of the election violence of 1917 was Mayor Thomas B. Smith (center). Shown is plainclothes officer George A. Eppley (top left), murdered trying to protect candidate James A. Carey (top right). Two of the Bronx gunmen are John "Lefty" Costello (bottom left) and Jacob "Butch" Mascia (bottom right).

CHAPTER *5*

The Frog Hollow Musketeers
Murder In "The Bloody Fifth"

I t's an arguable point, but no less an authority than Lincoln Steffens declared turn-of-the-century Philadelphia to be the "worst-governed city in the country." With 10,000 city workers paying kickbacks to the party and millions in city contracts at stake, the most corrupt, sordid machine politics prevailed.

Winning and maintaining control of City Hall meant that on Election Day no dirty trick was too foul, no low tactic too vile. Dead people voted by the thousands. Votes were purchased wholesale for as little as 25 cents and a mug of beer. Ballot boxes were stuffed and sometimes stolen. And in certain wards, violence was as integral to the election process as wall posters.

No place were intimidation, flying fists, flying bricks and flying bullets more in vogue than the Fifth Ward. Today we know the neighborhood as up-scale Society Hill, but the term "The Bloody Fifth" was even more popular and more accurate in the years between 1850 and 1920.

The Fifth's boundaries in 1917 were 7th Street to the Delaware River, Chestnut to South Street. It had pockets of poor blacks, many Jews and Irish and a few old-line families. The newspapers would never cease pointing out the irony that the corrupt and brutal Fifth "lies in the shadow of Independence Hall." It was where the politically inspired racial violence took the life of Octavius Catto (Chapter 2) and others as power shifted painfully from a Democratic machine to a Republican machine.

By 1917, the city's Democratic Party was a mere shell. The fight that year was between two equally odious and disreputable factions of the GOP machine. The primary contest unleashed unprecedented violence, even by the standards of the "Bloody Fifth."

Always in the past, the intimidation and brutality was handled by local bullies. But in 1917 the "Vare Faction" in the Fifth Ward opted to import an 18-man crew of gun-toting New York gangsters to handle the dirty work.

The result of the decision to contract out the strong-arm work had horrendous consequences and electrified even the notoriously blasé, apathetic citizenry of Philadelphia. It was a monumentally stupid decision that resulted in scores of cracked heads, an attempted assassination of a council candidate and the murder of a police detective. Not only were a score of gunmen, corrupt cops and political operatives arrested, tried and jailed, but for the first time, a Philadelphia mayor was put on trial in connection with a homicide and a grand jury called for the mayor's impeachment. On the positive side, the call went out for reform in one of the largest and most emotional mass meetings in city history.

Before delving into the mayhem of late September 1917, a bit of background is in order: At the time the competing Republican camps were headed by the South Philadelphia-based Vare brothers, Edwin, George and William, and by North Philadelphia-based James P. "Sunny Jim" McNichol and his ally State party boss U.S. Sen. Boies Penrose.

The Vares and McNichol were aptly labeled "the contractor bosses." It was an era when the City paid private contractors to perform many basic services, including trash collection and street repair. He who controlled City Hall controlled the contracts.

Thus the Vares, born on a humble South Philly pigfarm, collected $18 million in street cleaning contracts over the years. The ambitious brothers also controlled companies that built bridges, dug sewers and performed roadwork. In total the Vare interests landed 341 city contracts between 1888 and 1929 worth more than $28 million.

Sonny Jim's construction companies built the $25 million Torresdale water filtration plant, the Benjamin Franklin Parkway, Roosevelt Boulevard, subways and snagged endless street paving contracts. In addition, both McNichol and the Vares were handed many millions in contracts with gas, telephone and other public utilities—contracts that needed City Council approvals.

The Vares were particularly effective political players. In 1917 the majority of GOP ward leaders and councilmen and Mayor Thomas B. Smith were all allied with the canny Vares. But there was a hot battle between Vare and McNichol forces in the "Bloody Fifth." The major contest pitted Vare lieutenant Isaac "Ike" Deutsch against McNichol candidate James A. Carey. At stake was ward leadership and a seat on the Select Council.

In the weeks leading up to the election there had been tensions and trouble. McNichol people would say they had warned the mayor of pending trouble and asked for police protection. It was obvious there would be no protection from the cops in the neighborhood police station at 3rd and Delancey. All were Deutsch adherents. Twenty-six cops who would not pledge loyalty to the Vare machine found themselves walking a beat in the most remote parts of the city. A few quit the force in disgust.

The Ledger reported that the day before the election "squads of imported rowdies whose hip-pockets bulged ominously, paraded the streets all day, insulted pedestrians, many of whom were women, and in general made trouble at various places in the ward." The newspaper said police in the precinct were busy, but they weren't keeping order. The cops were out arresting key Carey workers on various trumped-up charges.

Finally, around 9 p.m. all hell broke loose at the Finletter Republican Club, 621 Spruce Street, headquarters of the Carey forces. Scores of people were inside the club preparing for the election when a shot was fired through a first-floor window, narrowly missing one man and lodging in a chair.

The shot was followed by an all-out assault. About 30 men rushed through the front door armed with blackjacks and bottles, attacking everyone in reach. According to the Ledger and witnesses, at least some of the raiders were plainclothes cops.

Someone in the club cried out, "The bulls are coming. Beat it!" There was a mad scramble for the rear door. Those who didn't make it out were whacked with blackjacks, kicked and trampled. One victim was identified as a crippled news dealer. Two of those beaten were off-duty policemen loyal to the McNichol faction. One had recently been transferred from the Fifth to Chestnut Hill. Four victims were taken to Pennsylvania Hospital for treatment.

The raid ended as suddenly as it began; someone whistled and the goons beat a quick retreat. In minutes uniformed police arrived, put out a riot call, but made no arrests.

One of those upstairs in the club during the attack was Assistant District Attorney Joseph H. Maurer who told reporters, "I've been living in the Fifth Ward since 1885. I never believed I would live to see such a scene as that deliberately pulled off last night." The next day Mauer would witness an even deadlier scene at close range and not escape unscathed.

The officer in charge of the police district, Lt. David Bennett, told reporters he knew nothing about the attack at the Finletter Club. He said he was in City Hall meeting with his superiors at the time. It would turn out that Bennett not only knew about the violence wracking his precinct but actually was orchestrating the lawlessness—and would eventually pay the price in prison.

On primary day September 19, Bennett's police were again out arresting leaders of the Carey faction and siding with Deutsch people everytime there was a dispute over the eligibility of a voter. Folks who were particularly observant might have noticed strangers roaming the polling places with small white ribbons in their lapels. Other men roaming the streets were plainclothes detectives from the vice squad. Their commander, obviously not a Vare man, detailed his men to the Fifth to help keep the peace.

In late morning Carey and Maurer were touring the polls. They were walking past 6th and Delancey, across from McCall Grammar School. Someone stepped out of a corner store and hollered, "That's him." Six to eight men wearing white ribbons exited the store and jumped the pair, beating them with blackjacks. Carey fell to the ground, blood streaming from his head. One man pulled a gun, pressed it to the candidate's head and pulled the trigger. It misfired.

A large number of uniformed policemen and plainclothesmen were nearby. The first to reach the scene was Detective George A. Eppley of the vice squad. One of the thugs turned his gun on the detective and fired twice. Eppley, a 30-year-old bachelor from West Philly, died on the spot. A black policeman, Clarence Hayden, rushed forward to arrest the bloody Carey. Other cops seemed to assist the gunmen make an escape. But vice squad detectives gave chase and nabbed two of the culprits.

It would soon be revealed that the killers were hired gangsters operating under the protection of precinct policemen. Detective Eppley, who would become a martyr to political reform, didn't know the tough guys with the small white ribbons and soft "Deutsch hats" had been turned loose on the Fifth with the promise of police immunity. The ribbons and hats identified them to Bennett's cops as friends.

The murder of a young cop by hired gunmen was too much even for the jaded citizens of the Quaker City. Dirty politics and rough campaign tactics were one thing: the importation of hired killers was beyond the pale.

The city's newspapers raised an unprecedented howl of outrage. Unlike earlier times, none of the major dailies were controlled by political machines. Despite the war raging in France, the Election Day lawlessness in the Bloody Fifth would dominate the front page of the Evening Bulletin, The Inquirer, The Record, the Ledger and The North American for the next few weeks.

Every newspaper was pointing a finger of blame at Mayor Smith and his top police officials. The moon-faced mayor, the owner of a bonding business, had been playing golf in Atlantic City on Election Day and was trying his best to sidestep the entire mess. "Deplorable. Very deplorable," was the only utterance reporters could coax from Smith on the murder.

Apparently, editors had little fear of libel suits. The headlines and reportage made no pretense of objectivity. "Smith's Gunmen Kill Detective in Fifth Ward. Policeman Victim of Mayor's Criminal Politics," blared the

North American before anyone but the two attackers were charged.

The North American ran scathing political cartoons of Smith on its front pages. The Record editorial page immediately declared, "The mayor is an open and daily lawbreaker." The Inquirer charged that "for days preceding the primary thugs of the Chief of Police of Philadelphia clubbed and battered heads and overran the streets of the Fifth Ward." And the Bulletin declared that the mayor must take the ultimate blame for the "Fifth Ward being terrorized, the police debased and the city shamed."

The two captured gunmen, John "Lefty" Costello and Jacob "Butch" Mascia, gave false addresses in the city and then said they were from Jersey City. Finally, they admitted they were from the Bronx. They came from a section known as Frog Hollow. The press was intrigued by the name and would often refer to the gunmen as "The Frog Hollow Musketeers."

Mascia quickly confessed to the actual killing. He said he was recruited by a man called "Little Neck." Investigators apparently misunderstood Mascia's accented English because the mysterious "Little Neck" turned out to be Nicholas "Little Nick" Ritt.

District Attorney Samuel Rotan, a Penrose man, quickly launched an investigation, pledging not to stop until he got the "big men" in the plot. The Bronx district attorney jumped into the investigation and soon arrested four members of the gang there. State Rep. Isadore Stern, a Carey ally who had been marked for attack but escaped with a black eye, didn't wait for Rotan. He pressed charges of conspiracy to commit murder against Mayor Smith, Deutsch and Police Lt. Bennett. All three were released under $10,000 bail.

Each day brought new revelations, new names, new intrigues. Carey, his head swathed in a turban of bandages, suffered a relapse. For a while his condition was critical. The magistrate who was issuing arrest warrants said he was followed by a suspicious-looking thug but had given him the slip by hailing a taxi. A black woman who had witnessed the shooting and could identify the gunmen said police were harassing her.

It was learned that 18 goons had been recruited in New York. They were put up in local hotels under phony names and hung out at Deutsch headquarters. At one point the gang gathered in Washington Square—truly in the shadow of Independence Hall—where a Deutsch operative issued each man a brand new blackjack. They were to be paid $15 a day. It was asserted that $1,000 was the total price for all the violence, including the assassination of Carey. All the hoodlums had police records and appropriate nicknames: "Straight Louis," "Whitey," "Butch," "Lefty," "Big Louie."

Seven days after the attack, a committee of businessmen, clergy and reformers organized a mass public meeting at the Academy of Music. The response was overwhelming. Three hundred VIPs sat on stage. Every auditorium seat was filled. Broad Street was so jammed in front of the Academy that those caught in the middle of the mob couldn't move.

Inside, a letter from John Wanamaker was read declaring the primary to be Philadelphia's "darkest day" since the assassination of Lincoln in 1865. The old merchant pleaded that his beloved city be "rescued and redeemed from the shame that threatens or has fallen upon it."

The Inquirer story on the gathering began on a melodramatic note: "Thou shalt not kill. These words hung in letters of palpitating fire in the proscenium of the Academy of Music last night. Thousands on thousands of persons crowded into the centre of the city to protest against the reign of misrule in Philadelphia and the orgy of bloodshed and terror in the Fifth Ward."

Five automobiles served as speakers' platforms for orators on the street. Inside, the most stirring speakers were former mayor Rudolph Blankenburg, a rare reform politician, affectionately known as "Old Dutch Cleanser," and Rev. Daniel I. McDermott of Old St. Mary's Catholic Church in the Fifth Ward. The fiery priest had branded Mayor Smith a murderer on the first day of the affair. His impassioned address and vivid Biblical imagery led to several loud standing ovations.

Blankenburg was cheered for three minutes before he could begin his address. "Never in my life have I seen such a crowd," declared the white-bearded reformer. "It is a crowd that typifies Philadelphia aroused. At last the Redemption Day of Philadelphia has come." Most important, a resolution was passed demanding the "impeachment or resignation from office of those public officials who shall be shown by the pending judicial investigation to have been neglectful of their duty."

The proclamation demanded that the police be taken out of politics and that "assessments or solicitation of contributions from policemen and other public employees for political purposes" end. Finally, the resolution called for the selection of a slate of independent candidates for the upcoming election.

The murder and its aftermath attracted national attention. The Literary Digest, sort of a Newsweek of its era, published an article declaring, "Philadelphia long a seething caldron of factional politics, now is facing one of the most scandalous and astounding upheavals in her history as the result of the murder of a police detective in the 'Bloody Fifth' ward on primary election day." Another magazine, The Independent, published an article on the situation under the headline "Government by Murder."

The legal maneuvering, charges, counter-charges and court proceedings went on until 1921. In less than three months, however, gunman Butch

Mascia was tried, found guilty of second–degree murder and given a minimum sentence of 15 years. He claimed he just fired in the air and accidentally hit Eppley. Other Frog Hollow Musketeers were convicted on lesser charges.

In the summer of 1918, Deutsch, Bennett and five other policemen connected to the election violence were tried in West Chester after obtaining a change of venue. Dozens of prosecution witnesses painted a fascinating picture of vicious politics Philadelphia-style in the Fifth with police as the key actors.

One of Chester County's longest court cases nearly ended in a mistrial when it was revealed that a juror had been approached with a bribe to vote for acquittal by an off-duty Philadelphia policeman. Astonished members of the Chester County bar reckoned this was the first jury-tampering incident in county history. The Bulletin said that "since the opening of the trial there have been a number of suspicious strangers seen in West Chester and the hometowns of the jurors." But Philadelphia DA Rotan "realizing the danger of jury-tampering" had dispatched "a corps of private detectives to West Chester to watch the movements of the jurors, those to whom they spoke and what they did."

The jury was not dismissed, and all defendants were convicted of conspiracy to prevent a free and fair election and given sentences ranging from six months to two years. In a grand demonstration of chutzpah, lawyers for the convicted men filed an appeal for a new trial, citing the fact that the juror who reported the bribe attempt had not been dismissed.

The story was back on the front pages during the eight-day trial of Mayor Smith in late January 1919. The conspiracy-to-murder charge had been downgraded by a judge to an alleged violation of the Shern Act, forbidding participation of city employees in politics and misdemeanors in office connected to Smith's actions during the primary election.

Again there was juicy testimony about police misconduct and dirty politics in the Fifth Ward. Some cops told how they were ordered to harass businessmen who were Carey supporters and chase away their customers. But there was not a lot that tied Smith to the dirty work. Some of the more interesting testimony came from "Little Nick" Ritt, leader of the Frog Hollow Musketeers, who claimed the cops not only pointed out Deutsch enemies to be attacked, but also staged his fake arrest after one assault. He was released five minutes after arriving at the police station.

Smith defense was that the police brass never relayed warnings about the brewing crisis in the Fifth. Yes, he had heard complaints from Stern and Carey and detailed his top detective to check it all out, but no negative report came back.

Police Superintendent James Robinson and other brass said everything appeared proper and orderly during their visits to the ward. Robinson said that after the raid on the Finletter Club, the mayor called him from Atlantic City to request an investigation and punishment for any police officers involved.

Smith spent six hours on the witness stand which included a grueling cross-examination by Assistant District Attorney Joseph A. Tulane, who would become a judge. The jury also heard a long parade of the mayor's character witnesses. During his lawyer's closing argument, the mayor cried loudly at the mention of his loving wife and small daughter.

Newspaper accounts of the trial made it appear that conviction was inevitable. In fact, Smith was quickly acquitted on the first ballot. A bitter Inquirer reporter wrote that when Smith's tears "unloosed the floodgates of self-pity . . . the jurors abandoned the evidence and, swayed only by sympathy and sentiment, brought in an acquittal." A few more trials followed for those in the private detective agency who had recruited the Frog Hollow gang.

Smith left politics after his term expired in 1920, but accepted an appointment to the Delaware River Bridge Commission, a notorious den of political patronage and contracting plums to this day. He died in 1949 at age 79.

Carey won the 1917 primary by less than 100 votes—despite the fact that the Deutsch forces ran off with one of the ballot boxes. He was later elected county sheriff. Maurer whose beating by the Frog Hollow thugs was less severe than Carey's, eventually became district attorney.

Never again were outside goons hired for election day duty in the Quaker City. And "The Bloody Fifth," now somewhat larger geographically, is today quite genteel.

The robbery of the Olney Bank & Trust branch took the life of off-duty policema Harry M. Cooper (center). Captured bandits are Joseph Curry (top left), Williar Juliano (top right), Frankie Doris (bottom left) and Harry Bentley (bottom right).

CHAPTER 6

A Posse Gets the Bad Guys
The Olney Bank Robbery

Just as in other cities, bank robberies in Philadelphia seem as numerous and mundane as house fires. But a few stand out either because of the derring-do of the thieves, their ingenuity, bloodshed, the size of the haul or the comedy of errors surrounding the heist.

What became famous as "The Olney Bank Robbery" of May 4, 1926, contained all those elements and more. Zaniness and tragedy blended in a scenario that seemed to follow the script of a Hollywood Western: a blazing shoot-out, a horse-chase involving a posse of heroic citizens, followed by swift justice and a legal lynching.

It was the era of bootleg booze and Philadelphia seemed awash in crime and violence. A plethora of thugs, petty hoodlums and swaggering gangsters, of the James Cagney variety, kept the police jumping and newspaper presses humming.

A sampling of local crime news in early May 1926 provides the flavor of the times. We read that "two colored suspects" have been released in the slaying of Mrs. Thomas J. Walsh inside her West Philadelphia house and that 18-year-old James McDevitt with "a sneer on his face," confessed to 20 armed holdups in six weeks, ending with a police shoot-out.

A high-speed chase of four young Jewish gangsters ended when the thugs' car overturned at 27th and Lehigh. Ex-boxer and dance hall manager Vincent Franchetti, also known as "Joe Jackson," was shot and killed on a sidewalk crowded with late-night diners and theater-goers at Broad and Spruce.

The Evening Bulletin's front page informed readers that Dr. E.A. Streckler of Philadelphia General Hospital believes "brain fever" (encephalitis) might be the cause of "widespread crime among the youth of today."

Former DA Samuel Rotan recommended a return of the whipping post during a speech before the Big Brothers Association. And police were "combing the underworld" for the five bandits who shot and killed the paymaster of a manufacturing firm on a busy Center City street just a block from a police station.

With such rampant crime and gangsterism, the Olney Bank & Trust Company naturally requested police protection when transferring large sums. And on that fateful and pleasant May morning, the bank at 5th and Tabor was sending $80,000 to the Federal Reserve. Enroute, another $20,000 would be added at the bank's Feltonville branch, a triangular piece of real estate at the juncture of Rising Sun Avenue, Wyoming Avenue and Mascher Street.

At 9:40 a.m. the sack containing $80,000 was picked up by bank messengers William Lee and William Miller and Patrolman Joseph Kaelin. It took only five minutes for the trio to arrive in Lee's car at the branch bank.

Lee parked at the curb while Miller went inside for the $20,000 pickup. Just as Miller was re-entering the car, a big blue Buick sedan pulled up, blocking the bank car. The Buick carried five gun-toting gangsters wearing stocking masks. They leapt out and pushed their guns through the windows of the bank car. One bandit let loose a shotgun blast directly into the car. Officer Kaelin was hit in the head and neck. One of the bandits reached inside the car and grabbed the bag with the $80,000. The thugs then piled back into the sedan.

Had they roared off with their loot, it would have gone down as one of the largest bank robberies in city history. But the perfect heist was about to be ruined by the appearance of foot patrolman Louis Pizzo. Newspapers would describe Pizzo as "short" or "diminutive," but he would soon prove to have a full measure of calm courage. Normally, Pizzo would have pulled the police box in front of the bank well before the robbery. But that morning he was late, and just in time to see the robbery go down.

Pizzo began blasting away at the bandits with his revolver and immediately disabled the gangsters' car. "My first shot blew out the tire of the car," he would recall. "The gang seemed excited, desperate, and they were firing in all directions. I emptied my gun and tried to draw their attention to me. I was afraid they would kill Kaelin and the bank messenger. I stepped behind a pole to reload and bullets were whizzing close by."

The injured Kaelin was now lying on the sidewalk, bleeding badly and trying to get to his pistol. The gunmen attempted to start their disabled car by pushing it. One lucky shot by Pizzo had torn through the car's hood and hit the distributor, killing the engine. While one masked bandit fired in all directions, the others pushed.

In the middle of a gunfight, a man stepped off a trolley at the intersection and strolled over to offer a hand to those he saw pushing the car. He got just close enough to realize they all wore masks and to become the target of their bullets.

Realizing they would never get the car started, the bandits took off on foot, turning to fire at the pursuing Pizzo. For unknown reasons they left the cash bag behind. Though he didn't know it, Pizzo had hit one stickup man in the leg. In the meantime, several citizens who had witnessed the shooting were swinging into action. The fleeing bandits would soon have a determined citizen-posse hot on their heels.

Three of the bandits were running south on Palethorpe Street when they spotted a horse-drawn milk wagon halted by the curb. The driver and a company supervisor were chatting on the sidewalk. The robbers pointed their guns at the startled milkmen and climbed aboard the wagon. Two gunmen moved to the rear of the wagon where they piled cartons and milk crates as a barricade. The third bandit began whipping the horse who took off at a gallop down Palethorpe. Little did the bandits know that the street led back to busy Rising Sun Avenue.

Back at the scene of the shooting an 18-year-old youth snatched up the cash bag with the $80,000. He refused to turn it over to messenger Miller, so they marched together into the bank with the cash.

The shooting was witnessed by gas company workers who were laying a new main on Rising Sun Avenue. Charles McCready and Howard Jayne decided to follow the bandits in their company truck. A spectator found a shotgun on the floor of the bandits' stalled getaway car and gave it to McCready.

The gunfire attracted the attention of off-duty policeman Harry M. Cooper, 45, who was relaxing with his wife and five-month-old baby, Harry Jr., on the porch of his home at 4606 Rising Sun Avenue. "He took one glance toward the bank, rushed upstairs and got his pistol," his widow told reporters. "His last words were, 'Keep the baby in the house. The bank is being robbed. I'll be right back.'"

Auto mechanic George Stark decided to enter the chase in his Hudson touring car. He picked up two strangers, Walter Miller, a 23-year-old poultry salesman, and David M. Rittenhouse, an armed off-duty night watchman at an Olney factory.

But the citizen who would prove the most intrepid, Fred H. Loscamp (also spelled Loskamp by the newspapers), was inside the bank transacting business when all hell broke loose. The garage owner watched Pizzo shooting it out with the gang and was itching to get his hands on a weapon. As soon as the bandits had scattered, Loscamp found a woman who said there was a pistol in her house. He was following her home when another woman got into the act.

Loscamp testified, "While I was going after this first lady some other lady leaned out of a second-floor window and said, 'I have a gun.' I said, 'Let's have it.' She threw me an automatic pistol and a clip of cartridges. I caught the pistol, but I dropped the clip.

"As I turned back to pick up the clip, one of the men crossing Palethorpe Street took a shot at me. I ran up Palethorpe Street toward Rising Sun Avenue, where I jumped on the side [running board] of a touring car." Loscamp was picked up by Stark and his two determined companions. Officer Cooper would soon hop aboard the gas truck. Both vehicles would tail the milk wagon as the air hummed with flying bullets.

Even before Cooper got on the truck, the gas company guys spotted one of the gunmen on the street. McCready leapt out of the truck and tackled the armed bandit. The two-fisted gasman was aided in the apprehension by an iceman. He arrived on the scene brandishing an ice pick (according to one newspaper) or, more likely, a fearsome ax used to break up 300-pound blocks of ice. Whether an ice pick or ax, it was enough to convince the badman to give up his weapon.

Pizzo, that short but fearless cop, captured another outlaw. Some accounts say the man jumped off the milk wagon and Pizzo nabbed him. Other newspapers have the stealthy bandit trying to backtrack and suddenly coming face-to-face with the pursuing cop. There is no question, however, that Pizzo was out of ammunition at this point while the bandit was still armed. Using all his strength the little cop leapt at the outlaw, smashing his empty gun into the bandit's jaw. Pizzo broke a finger, but his attack took the fight out of the bandit.

Back to the chase: The milk wagon, now with two desperadoes on board, was careening south with the gas truck and the Hudson touring car in hot pursuit. Loscamp would later testify, "The shooting was terrific. Volley after volley was exchanged between the milk wagon and the cars in the chase. . . . We were 35 to 40 feet behind the milk wagon at the time and the UGI [United Gas Improvement] truck was between us and the milk wagon. By this time I could plainly see the two men in the milk wagon who were shooting at the truck with the policeman in it."

Jayne, the driver of the UGI truck, told what happened next: "Shots were fired at my car from behind a barricade of boxes in the milk wagon. Glass was shattered in my windshield by bullets. I passed the other cars and got within 25 feet of the rear of the milk wagon. We came to the dead end of Bristol Street at the intersection of 2nd and Rising Sun.

"The men in the milk wagon were whipping up their horse, and two revolvers were discharged from the right side of the wagon at my car. I told the policeman [Cooper] to shoot the horse as a means of stopping the bandits.

"As Cooper was taking aim to shoot the horse, there was a shot [actually two shots] from the milk wagon and the policeman fell over my shoulder. When Cooper fell, I saw two holes in his left temple.

"In the meantime, the men in the milk wagon—still whipping up their horse—drove over the bridge and down Rising Sun Avenue. I sped up, holding Cooper whom I thought was mortally wounded, by the belt. And I drove past the milk wagon. As I did so, I received a volley of fire. The bullets broke the rest of the glass in my truck.

"I continued on 5th Street in the hope of finding a policeman on traffic duty, but I found none. And when I looked back, I saw two men firing from the milk wagon at the other cars in the rear. I drove my car across the tracks at 5th Street in hopes of heading off the milk wagon. I got out and barricaded myself behind an ice cream wagon and began firing as the milk wagon approached. I fired two shots and forced the bandits to turn north on 5th Street.

"Then I realized it was my duty to take the policeman to a hospital as quickly as I could," said the gas worker. "I took him to the Samaritan Hospital but he was dead."

One policeman was badly wounded, and one dead. Two robbers had been captured. One bandit had disappeared and was never identified. The gas company truck was out of the chase. The two gunmen in the milk truck were still racing south. Presumably, the horse was exhausted.

Stark's touring car with the armed and determined Loscamp on board was not giving up. They chased the wagon to where it was abandoned, more than a mile from the bank. The gunmen dashed off on foot with Loscamp and his posse in hot pursuit. By now police were beginning to stream into the area.

At this juncture, Frederick Baker was enjoying a leisurely breakfast at 3623 N. Percy Street while his wife, Elsie, washed dishes. The front door had been left open for the laundryman to pick up some bundles. Suddenly two masked, gun-toting thugs burst into the house. "Don't move, lady, and keep your mouth shut," one told the woman. Her husband was also threatened. The gunmen exited through a rear door and dashed down an alley.

From her rear window, neighbor Mary Kreitter saw the two men leave the Baker house with drawn guns and feared her neighbors had just been killed. She dashed outside to where one man had just exited the alley and the second was following. "I had no weapon but a broom, and I braced the ends of it across the alley," she told reporters. "He ran at me, pushed me aside and ran into 9th Street."

The first gunman didn't get far. At 8th and Erie he ran directly into

Loscamp. As the robber raised his pistol, Loscamp pushed his borrowed automatic in the bandit's face. "All right you got me. Let go of my arm," declared the captured tough. Loscamp kept one hand on the robber's arm and his gun in his face until Stark arrived with a policeman. The second gunman who had passed through the Bakers' house was caught minutes later by police.

The fifth robber had gone off in the direction of Roosevelt Boulevard and would forever remain a mystery man. But the four bandits turned out to be familiar faces to the cops. "They were all professional gunmen," The Inquirer informed readers.

Loscamp had snared the gang's leader, Joseph Curry, a Kensington tough associated with "The Eggers Gang," whose members had been arrested in Philadelphia for killing a federal marshal in San Francisco. They were returned to the West Coast for trial, where Curry was tried and acquitted.

The tall galoot who hobbled through the Bakers' house along with Curry was Harry Bentley. Officer Pizzo had nabbed William Juliano, who was also being sought for the murder of a gangster known as "Dopey Pete." Gasman McGready had captured Frank "Tenderloin Frankie" Doris, who had made headlines in 1922 when he shot and killed another man in the apartment of a cabaret singer. A jury found the slaying by "dope user" Doris was self-defense. Just the year before, 1925, Doris was arrested for a $5,000 payroll holdup but released when the witness who had identified him on two occasions suddenly lost his memory. All the suspects were bruised and bandaged when hauled before a magistrate, from rough handling by the cops or by the citizen-posse.

The failed stickup had been sensationally weird and the aftermath would prove just as unique. The public and press were outraged, and authorities seemed determined to set a record for speedy trials. The attempted robbery had taken place on a Tuesday. On Wednesday it took a grand jury 10 minutes to indict the quartet on 30 separate counts, including the murder of Cooper. Curry's trial was set for Monday and it kicked off right on schedule.

All four bandits would be represented in separate trials by Philadelphia's most renowned and eccentric criminal defense lawyer, C. Stuart "Chippy" Patterson Jr., and his colleague Louis F. McCabe. Patterson was truly a one-of-a-kind personality and living legend. The 1960 bestseller *The Worlds of Chippy Patterson* by Arthur H. Lewis is one of the finest and most fascinating biographies ever written about a Philadelphian. The delightfully odd lawyer rejected his patrician family and identified totally with society's outcasts and miscreants. From 1907 to 1933, he defended 401 accused murderers, compiling an acquittal rate near 50 percent. Only eight Patterson clients ever paid for murder with their lives—four were the Olney bank bandits.

The trials received tight police security as witnesses received telephone threats and rumors spread that the underworld would try to spring the gang. One newspaper claimed gangsters were shaking down merchants in the Tenderloin for a legal defense fund. Another story said "every gunman, bandit, bootlegger and gambling house owner as well as every man whose name has been linked with the underworld in the past" was asked to contribute $50 for the men on trial.

Certainly, one of those threatened was Loscamp who took the witness stand, calmly returning Curry's stare until the gangster dropped his eyes. Loscamp not only captured the gang's leader but also was the sole witness who could positively identify Curry as the gunman who killed Cooper. The point was moot, however, since anyone involved in a crime resulting in a homicide can be convicted of murder regardless of who pulls the trigger.

The trials in the quaintly named Court of Oyer and Terminer, were the first under a new Pennsylvania statute giving the jury the responsibility of setting the punishment in first-degree murder convictions at either life in prison or death by electrocution.

One trial followed another with only a few days hiatus for preparation by Patterson and Assistant DA Maurice J. Speiser. Bentley was the only defendant to take the stand and offer an alibi: He was out shopping for his mother and somehow got a bullet in his leg and arrested by mistake. Mom swore it was true. That's not all. Bentley showed the jury that his right thumb and most of his right index finger were missing. So how could he fire a gun? The jury took a full night to return the verdict, but no one believed Bentley's tale. The delay was due to debate over life or death for the gunman.

The gangsters accepted the death verdicts in style, all feigning a tough nonchalance, with the exception of Tenderloin Frankie Doris. He seemed to be losing his mind. Patterson's defense (and later appeals) for Doris was based on the argument that he was captured before Cooper was shot and killed. It didn't work. When the death penalty was announced, Doris' "red-rimmed eyes rolled in terror and he gasped for breath . . . making no effort to wipe away the tears that streamed down his cheeks." The press reported that a juvenile court judge had once warned Doris, "You are the type of criminal whose life ends in the electric chair. Take my warning and go straight."

Five weeks after the botched stickup, the trials were complete and four hoodlums, all in their 20s, were waiting on Death Row. Patterson desperately filed fruitless appeals and made a herculean effort to have the sentences commuted to life. He was a man with boundless compassion for the underdog, and his biographer believes the lawyer's slide into ill health began with the execution of the four Olney Bank Bandits.

Ten months after the shoot-em-up on Rising Sun Avenue, the four kept their appointment with the Pennsylvania electric chair. Two days prior to the execution, Patterson visited to say farewell. Doris was practically out of his mind. But Juliano and Bentley had something to get off their chests. They said a man named Matthew Overnack, convicted of bank robbery in Westmont, N.J., was actually innocent. They were there, and Overnack was not. Patterson believed the pair and so did a deputy prison warden. But it took New Jersey authorities six years to relent and grant the unlucky inmate his freedom.

The Philadelphia press provided full details of the quartet's last hours on March 7, 1927. Wiseguy Curry's last request was for a pair of rollerskates. Bentley wanted to hear a song called "It's That Old Pal of Mine"; he said it made him think of his father. An inmate from another part of the prison who knew the song was fetched and sang the tune. The Inquirer wrote, "Even the guards were touched by the poignancy of the occasion as the lines of the ballad rose sobbingly in the narrow corridor of the death house."

On his cell wall Bentley wrote, "This is No Man's Land." Juliano drew a heart with his name and date under it. Even Doris scribbled his name in his cell. We learn that Doris, who wouldn't speak to the others, ate a hardy breakfast while the others nibbled. Catholic chaplain Rev. B.A. O'Hanlon walked the proverbial "Last Mile" with the men. It took two jolts to dispatch Juliano. In 30 minutes all four were dead.

We learn that Officer Cooper's widow was away from home that day because so many friends and relatives of the condemned men had beseeched her to contact the governor and ask that he spare the lives of the bandits. In addition to the Coopers' new baby, there were four daughters. A fund promoted by the newspapers raised $20,000 for the family.

Following the executions, the Bulletin ran a photo of a Kensington street jammed wall-to-wall with those attending Curry's funeral. He had become a neighborhood legend.

A gangland war broke out a month after the executions. Some police believed the failure to rescue the bandits was behind the bloodshed. Gangster Edward Regan was arrested in connection with a double gangland slaying while driving Curry's old roadster. Regan told the cops he was scheduled to marry Curry's widow, Aggie, in a few hours.

About the same time, police raided the house of Frankie Doris where they arrested his widow, Gertie, and several guests on drug charges.

Neighbors said the place was an infamous opium den. Labeled a "Gangland Queen" by the press, Mrs. Doris was arrested from time-to-time in coming years for a variety of offenses, including safecracking. However, she earned a new nickname, "Salvation Gert," when she vowed to reform and became a soldier of the Lord in the Salvation Army.

Principal plotters in the murderous "Arsenic Ring" are Herman (left) and cousin Paul Petrillo. In the center is Morris "Evil Eye" Bolber.

CHAPTER 7

A Fantastical Cabal of Killers
The Arsenic Ring

The use of the words "fantastic" and "fantastical" seemed to be mandatory in almost every newspaper story written from 1938 through 1941 about the cabal of oddball murderers who dispatched somewhere between 20 and 100 victims in order to collect on life insurance.

What became known as "The Arsenic Ring" was one of those stranger-than-fiction stories with a cast of characters kooky enough to make the burghers of Twin Peaks seem bland and normal by comparison. Just for starters, the Ring's leaders included a Talmudic "witch doctor;" a dapper spaghetti salesman/counterfeiter; a short, pudgy tailor who was the Ring's resident Casanova; and a "witch" who poisoned her husband, stepson and a boarder in her house.

Minor players included a once-wealthy obstetrician who pleaded guilty to participating in a murder that netted him $200, and a pants presser who poisoned his pregnant wife. The press dubbed wives involved in the poison plots the "Arsenic Widows." One woman who was on her fifth husband was called "The Kiss of Death."

Many victims were immigrants with menial jobs whose lives were sacrificed for as little as $2,500 in insurance money and rarely more than $10,000. In most cases, the Ring purchased several small policies on the victim. These "industrial" policies required no medical examination and usually had an $800 limit. Premiums in nickels and dimes were paid every two weeks. In one case, the Ring applied for 14 policies on the same victim. Eleven policies were granted. Five were sold by the same company through the same agent during a three-month period. While no agents were charged with crimes, several suspected what was happening. They excused any passive involvement with the rationalization that they were under pressure to sell insurance.

Most often, it was a wife who slipped poison into her spouse's food or drink and split the insurance money with the Ring's leaders. Sometimes a husband murdered a wife. And one guy dispatched his mother-in-law for a cut of $2,500. Some victims were down-and-out loners insured by the Ring and then murdered.

Arsenic compounds that brought on what seemed to be the symptoms of pneumonia were the weapon of choice. But more strenuous forms of execution were also employed, particularly if there was a double-indemnity clause in the policy for accidental death. So, one victim died in a staged hit-and-run auto accident and two were drowned. One of those sent to the bottom was a defenseless cripple pushed into the Schuylkill River. The second drowning victim was taken for a fishing trip off Sea Isle City, N.J., and tossed overboard by his new fishing "buddies."

While the majority of conspirators and victims were Italian-Americans, an admirable ecumenical spirit of teamwork reigned. There were also Jewish killers and victims. Two victims had Slavic surnames, and another hailed from Brazil.

Over a two-year period, the ring—like the proverbial onion—unpeeled layer-after-layer. The number of deaths and those involved wowed the public and even astonished investigators. It was quite an enterprise with a South Philadelphia Branch and a North Philadelphia/Germantown Branch. At one point, the district attorney set up a stadium-size scoreboard to keep track of the bodies, defendants, prosecutors and judges. In September 1939 eight trials of Ring members were scheduled for the same week.

Before it was over 26 people were indicted for murder. Three were acquitted. Two died in the electric chair. Fifteen were handed life sentences, including two women condemned to death whose sentences were commuted by the governor. The others received prison terms of varying lengths.

The actual number of those murdered is open to speculation because those who seemed to know everything never made complete confessions. And the killing went on for at least seven years. The earliest murders police could pin down dated to 1932. The first arrests didn't come until September 1938.

As if the facts were not sensational enough, the cops and the press engaged in an orgy of wild speculation. The Evening Bulletin declared, "How many victims will never be known. Police set a conservative total of 100, a 'probable' at 200 and a 'possible' at 300."

Perhaps. But these guesses seem wildly inflated, since only 21 deaths were actually proven in court. The investigation sparked a sort of hysteria that led to the wholesale disinterment of bodies. Several totally innocent people were held and later released. Law enforcement agencies in Camden,

Upper Darby and Hammonton, N.J., started digging up bodies and analyzing the cadavers for signs of poisoning. At one point, Philadelphia Coroner Charles H. Hersch angrily banned "fishing expeditions in graveyards" unless the district attorney could furnish solid proof of a crime. The coroner's outburst followed the arrests of three men who were soon cleared when autopsies showed no signs of foul play.

The originators and prime movers in the ring were first cousins: Paul and Herman Petrillo. Paul Petrillo was a tailor whose shop at Passyunk and Moore was "Arsenic Central," the place where most of the planning and scheming took place. Like several in the Ring, the slick, nattily-dressed tailor had a sideline business in the occult. The 45-year-old Petrillo could place curses on enemies, remove the "Evil Eye," provide amulets and ointments. He was also a very successful gigolo. Most of his black magic clientele were superstitious immigrant women and some became Petrillo's lovers. Of course Paul also had a wife and seven children.

Cousin Herman was noted for his dapper dress and flashy cars. He lived in Langhorne and worked, ostensibly, as a wholesale salesman of spaghetti and olive oil. Herman Petrillo's sideline was passing counterfeit $5s and $10s in the Philadelphia area. It was a Secret Service investigation into Petrillo's bogus bills that led to the serendipitous exposure of the murder-for-insurance ring.

The most colorful and memorable character in the incredible cast was bombastic Morris "Evil Eye" Bolber, also known as "The Rabbi." The stocky Jewish immigrant was labeled as either "a faith healer" or "witch doctor" by an infatuated press corps. Bolber was a full-time seer and mystic, with an office near 9th and Passyunk. Although no one in the Ring talked more to authorities—you couldn't shut Bolber up once he started—his role is not entirely clear. It appears that the garrulous master of the black arts was allied with the Petrillos from the start and shared in a lot of the Ring's profits. He was a man capable of pleading guilty to murder, and at the same time vehemently asserting that he never murdered anyone.

Again, those seeking advice, spells, potions and cures from Bolber were mostly women. Many were dissatisfied or angry with husbands who were running around with other women. Bolber could supply love potions and spells to break up such affairs. He apparently steered women capable of poisoning their husbands to Paul Petrillo.

A fourth major player was weird, dumpy Carina Favato, another Evil-Eye expert, whom the press quickly labeled "The Witch Woman." She was charged with killing her common-law husband, her 18-year-old stepson and at least one boarder in her house. The Witch was also a baseball fan who put the hex on visiting teams playing the Philadelphia Athletics. A two-fisted witch, Favato attacked a male co-defendant while the pair was being questioned by police. She hung a whopping shiner on the poor guy that totally closed his eye. Favato's sideline business was bootlegging.

The crew of killers also included a powerfully built 250-pound thug nicknamed "Jumbo," an ally of Favato and alleged Mafia tough guy who spent half his life in Italian and American prisons.

The Ring came to light when the federal counterfeiting investigation focused in on Herman Petrillo. A federal informant purchased phony money from the spaghetti salesman and befriended dapper Herman with the hope of tracking down the source of the bogus bills. Petrillo offered the agent a surprise opportunity to make extra money. He said he would pay $500 in good cash or $2,500 in counterfeit bills if his new friend would murder some poor slob in Port Richmond. The informant feigned interest.

If possible, Petrillo wanted the killing to look like an accident. He suggested slugging the guy over the head with a sandbag, because it would leave no marks, and then tossing the chap down the steps. Alternatively, the hitman might want to take the victim for a ride and then run him over. The intended victim was 38-year-old Ferdinand Alfonsi. Apparently his wife was in on the plot and would hang a towel outside their house to signal the killer that her husband was home alone.

Several times the would-be killer offered excuses for delaying the hit. Finally, Petrillo informed him that the deal was off. He said Alfonsi was now in the hospital with enough arsenic in his guts to kill a dozen men. At this point, the feds informed Philadelphia police. Petrillo and Mrs. Alfonsi were arrested. The victim never knew it, but his life had been insured for $7,000. He lingered awhile in great pain before dying.

At this point in October 1938 it was a simple case of a single murder and two defendants. But an insurance agent recognized Herman Petrillo's photo in the newspapers as a man he had seen in the home of Carina Favato. The agent had visited the Witch's house to insure her teen-age stepson. Now the kid was dead. And several members of her household had also passed on to a better place. Something was fishy. Sam Riccardi, a very determined detective, is credited with pushing for the disinterment of several long-dead bodies; and soon the investigation was flowering beyond the cops' wildest imagination.

Herman Petrillo was the first Ring member tried, in March 1939. He was quickly convicted and sentenced to death. It was the near-certainty of earning a place in line for a seat in Pennsylvania's electric chair which convinced so many others to plead guilty in return for a life sentence.

A key witness at the trials of Herman and Paul Petrillo was Paul's nephew from New York. The saga of John Cacopardo is as "fantastical" as anything to emerge from the Arsenic Ring.

At the time of the trials, the tall, lanky Cacopardo was an inmate in Sing-Sing Prison serving a 30-year-to-life sentence for killing his sweetheart in a Brooklyn apartment in late 1936. The eyewitness whose testimony sent Cacopardo to the Big House was his own Uncle Paul. Now it was payback time. Cacopardo was transported to Philadelphia where he would recall how Uncle Paul tried on several occasions to recruit him to commit homicide for $500 a pop. It would be easy: just slip a powder into some guy's beer when he wasn't looking. Cacopardo testified that he had wanted no part of the action. However, Herman, too, urged the young man to get in on the easy money.

It was good testimony, but Cacopardo had another wild story. He was now saying that it wasn't he who pulled the trigger and killed his lover, Molly Starace. The killer was Uncle Paul. The nephew said he was struggling with Petrillo for a gun when it went off —several times—killing poor Molly. And the whole crazy episode was related to a proposed arsenic poisoning of Molly's well-insured stepfather.

It seems that Molly had been married and divorced three times in her young life and felt certain her ill luck was the result of the Evil Eye. While a skeptic himself, Cacopardo took her to Philadelphia on several occasions to consult with Uncle Paul, a specialist in removing curses. To make a long story short, Petrillo had sent a letter to Molly proposing sending her stepfather "on a trip to California," which was his code for murder. The letter hinted that John would help out in the endeavor.

Cacopardo said that on the night of killing he was trying to get the letter from Molly, either to warn the stepfather or protect himself or to talk sense to Molly. Petrillo was in another room and entered the bedroom where Cacopardo and Molly were arguing. The evil uncle pulled a gun and threatened his nephew. A struggle for the gun ensued, and Molly was killed.

According to Cacopardo's story, after the shots, Petrillo urged him to flee. Everyone would think John was the shooter. Petrillo had a lot of influence and would fix things. Fearing his uncle and expecting him to offer helpful testimony, Cacopardo took the rap and never mentioned the "struggle-over-the-gun" story. Instead of helping his case, Uncle Paul's testimony was devastating.

That was Cacopardo's strange tale and he went on telling it for years with no results. In prison he found religion and became a chaplain's assistant. With the aid of a Presbyterian minister and new lawyers, the mysterious letter was found. A New York judge believed his tale and ordered his release. A higher court then reversed the judge, but Gov. Thomas E. Dewey granted Cacopardo a pardon. In 1957 he was ordained as a Presbyterian minister. The inspirational story of the innocent man who spent 15 years in prison for a murder committed by his uncle was told—with various degrees of accuracy—by many newspapers and magazines.

But the star of this freak show was Morris Bolber, who contemptuously dismissed his fellow witches and black magic practitioners as mere dilettantes. Bolber had quit the faith healing game about a year before the first arrests. He was located after the first round of trials in Brooklyn, where he was operating a grocery store.

Bolber loved the limelight. He not only testified at several trials and provided police with more than a dozen new leads, but even produced a five-part series on his amazing life and accomplishments for The Inquirer. Actually, the faith healer's self-serving mishmash of half-truths and pure baloney was told through reporter Owen F. McDonnell.

"I have healed men, women and children throughout the world by faith," he declared. "Virtually, all the thousands I have treated, more than 20,000 in Philadelphia alone, I have helped to health and happiness. I have read the ancient mysteries of the Kabala. I have seen what is called witchcraft drive mental devils into oblivion."

Bolber portrayed himself as a child genius who entered Grodno University at age nine. As a student at a religious school in Odessa, the great healer was introduced to the mysteries of the Kabala. He wandered the world. He learned to speak 10 languages. He spent five years in a hut in "Chongogo, China" as an acolyte of "the Chinese sorceress Rino." The wrinkled, old wisewoman taught Bolber secret words and incantations and how to heal the sick. Most important, Rino introduced her pupil to "the secret of the knife."

"The knife," Rino would say, "is the instrument of witchcraft. As the painter needs his brush, as the physician needs the stethoscope, so we need the knife. By using it, by waving it, by uttering certain words, it will perform many miracles."

The Italian version of the black arts is called *Fatura,* said Bolber. And he first met Paul Petrillo in 1932 at a conclave of *Fatura* practitioners in South Philadelphia. He claimed Petrillo started sending him clients in return for a 50 percent cut of all fees. He hotly declared that the tailor was jealous of his powers and tried hard to steal his secrets.

In the series, Bolber told how he would clean a house of the evil spirits, charging as much as $75. But on the witness stand, Bolber confessed to putting a frog in the basement of a client. Sure enough, Bolber was successful in cleansing the house of evil spirits making noise in the dark basement. He simply removed the frog.

Bolber once convinced simple-minded Ring member, Salvatore

Sortino—the guy who along with Herman Petrillo pushed the crippled victim into the Schuylkill—to carry an egg under his armpit for nine days and nine nights. The special egg would then hatch a devil. The egg was protected by a cloth and the arm placed in a sling. On the last day, Sortino was to walk around a graveyard with outstretched arms and then sit in his basement and wait until the devil appeared. The judge didn't believe the tale. Bolber took the witness stand to confirm it really happened and spelled out all the details in the Inquirer series. Bolber also volunteered the information that he had chanted Chinese incantations over a pair of Sortino's socks for luck.

Witchcraft is real and works for those who believe in it, declared Bolber. But it does not work for non-believers.

Bolber was unstoppable on the witness stand. Once he got talking, neither lawyers nor judges had much luck in halting or controlling the torrent of words accompanied by histrionic gestures. The Evening Bulletin published an analytical portrait of the Witch Doctor by a Temple professor of psychiatry who observed Bolber's courtroom antics. The professor labeled the mystic a "megalomaniac" and a "morbid egoist" who "seems to find his deepest satisfaction in self-expansion."

Bolber's bravura performance was just one act in the mesmerizing sideshow unfolding in the courtrooms in City Hall. Herman Petrillo tried to attack the jury after he was sentenced to death. A daughter of one of the victims lunged at Paul Petrillo. One male defendant had a total mental breakdown in court. One "Arsenic Widow" charged with murder, attempted suicide three times.

Ring leader Paul Petrillo was executed on March 31, 1941. Herman Petrillo died in the same electric chair at Bellefonte, October 20, 1941. The dapper spaghetti vendor said, "Gentlemen, you are about to witness the execution of an innocent man". A moment before the switch was pulled he mumbled, "I want to see the governor."

Evil Eye Bolber was rewarded for his cooperation with a life sentence and was constantly filing for release from prison. He said he wanted to go to Israel. The Rabbi's efforts were for naught; he died of natural causes at Eastern State Penitentiary in February 1954.

One of those arrested in 1938 was Josephine Sadita, another *Fatura* healer and purveyor of magic potions, who was suspected in the death of one victim and, perhaps, as many as three. A mother of five who was once convicted of shooting her husband, Sadita was released under $2,500 bail and instantly disappeared.

Memories of the murderous ring were rekindled when she surrendered in 1945. The short, swarthy suspect had been working on farms in Virginia.

But the key witness who had pointed the finger of guilt at Sadita had served her time and vanished. Other witnesses were hard to locate after seven years. The DA was forced to drop the murder charge. Instead she was convicted of practicing medicine without a license and did a year in prison.

It was an interesting tale. Sadita had treated a South Philadelphia man for ulcers back in 1938, and her patient testified at a magistrate's hearing. Alphonse DeJesse said that before Sadita would do anything he had to turn over all his money, $156. Then the healer—dressed in a dirty "magic" coat—wrapped two rabbitskins around his stomach and uttered the magic words, "Aska wanna, jinksa, hoo." She then took some empty eggshells, placed a few drops of the patient's blood in them and hung the shells over his bed, muttering the same incantation. DeJesse said nine days later he felt no better and the rabbitskins were starting to stink.

Sadita was summoned to his bedside. She removed the skins, took another $112 and gave him "medicine" which made him feel even worse. Suspicious police analyzed the contents of the bottle and discovered it was merely some flavored grain alcohol.

Sadita's arrest pretty much ended the saga of The Arsenic Ring. But not quite. In April 1950 a body with three bullets in his head was tossed from a car at 10th and Christian streets. Police identified the man as Peppe Ulongo. They had been seeking him for years in connection with the Arsenic Ring. The cops then questioned and released a woman identified as the dead man's girlfriend. Her name was Josephine Sadita.

Corrine Sykes was the last woman executed in Pennsylvania.

CHAPTER 8

Rush to the Electric Chair
Corrine Sykes

It was a relatively routine homicide in late 1944. A black maid had brutally murdered her white employer with a kitchen knife. Theft was the motive. After first denying any involvement, the young woman signed a full confession.

In Philadelphia race is never irrelevant, and the case of Corrine Sykes stirred strong emotions. In fact, the young woman became a potent and enduring symbol for both whites and blacks.

In 1944 thousands of Philadelphia households employed black maids and cleaning women. A widely-held opinion was that you must watch these girls (they were always "girls" no matter how advanced their age) or they would steal you blind. Corrine Sykes was frightening proof of that prejudice. For not only had the cleaning girl stolen from her employer but viciously murdered that nice woman.

For blacks there was a feeling that Sykes was being rushed to the electric chair by a vengeful legal system acting a lot like a lynch mob. Sykes was mentally slow, easily led and seemed somehow to be an innocent dupe. There was real sympathy for Sykes among many domestic workers and resentment toward the white women who worked them hard, paid them low, watched them like hawks and treated them coldly.

In fact, there were feelings of sympathy throughout the black community for the young girl and her hard-working, religious family. She became the last woman executed in Pennsylvania. After her death, unshakable legends grew up around the case. Today there are thousands of African-Americans who have forgotten the details of the crime but are sure Corrine Sykes was innocent. Many are certain that the victim's husband confessed on his deathbed to the slaying. They are certain that they read the story of the deathbed confession in a newspaper, but no one can produce the clipping.

The murder happened on December 7, 1944. Sykes had been hired just two days before the killing by the Wodlinger family of Camac Street in Oak Lane. The 20-year-old maid was hired through an employment agency. She used the name of a woman on a stolen Social Security card and supplied a phony reference. She assumed the new identity to hide a criminal record. Sykes had been released in May 1944 after serving 11 months in jail for stealing jewelry from another employer.

Alone in the house with 45-year-old Freeda Wodlinger, the maid allegedly used a carving knife from the kitchen to slay the woman in the second-floor bathroom. The victim was stabbed several times in the chest and slashed across the face and left hand, severing the little finger. The maid then took $50 in cash, three rings and a furpiece.

Fingerprints in the house provided detectives with the maid's true identity. It was learned that she had left the city with her boyfriend, James C. "Jayce" Kelly, a 40-year-old bootlegger and luncheonette owner. They had gone to a hotel in New Jersey after the slaying, but two days later Kelly and Sykes were both arrested in North Philly.

Questioned by detectives, Sykes was soon telling conflicting stories, putting the blame on various men, including Kelly. Finally she admitted, "Nobody was with me. I did it all alone." Then she disavowed that confession and again pointed the finger of blame at Kelly. A few days later, she did sign a confession.

To her sympathizers, all this vacillation pointed to the fact that others were involved and the slow-witted maid was left to take the entire rap. Kelly insisted he knew nothing of the murder until he read about it in the newspaper. But there was enough evidence to charge him as an accessory after the fact and with receiving stolen goods.

Sykes' lawyer was Raymond Pace Alexander, one of the city's most prominent African-Americans—who would go on to become the first black city councilman and the first black judge of Common Pleas Court.

The judge was Vincent A. Carroll, a hard-nosed, "hanging judge" who often appeared to defense attorneys to be part of the prosecution's team. The trial was set for the end of January 1945—a little more than a month after the killing. Carroll ordered a delay, however, when three psychiatrists agreed that Sykes was suffering from "hysteria." Their report talked about a "mental condition" and "low intelligence."

The Philadelphia Tribune, the city's premier black newspaper, ran an article under the wishful headline "Death Penalty Unlikely for Maid in Murder Case." It was more editorial than news story and seemed to express the feelings of many African-Americans. The story declared, "Corrine Sykes has been on the lips and minds of thousands of people all over the country. . . . Murder under some circumstances is not murder. And while practically everyone would want to see the punishment fitted to the crime, in this particular case, folks who are still HUMAN, would not want to see punishment meted out where TREATMENT is needed.

"...If white men appointed to examine a Negro girl charged with murdering a WHITE woman agree she is suffering a mental condition that prevents her from being interrogated, you may be sure it is true!"

The Tribune writer makes much of Corrine's allegedly low intelligence declaring, "the fact stares us in the face that a SUBNORMAL CHILD and NOT A WOMAN committed what we smugly say is 'atrocious crime' not knowing that the accused murderer can not even write the word." The headline over Sykes' photo declared: "Low-Grade Mind." The caption read "CORRINE SYKES physically an adult, mentally a child."

That was one view; but there was cynicism among prison officials, who believed Sykes was faking hysteria. In any case, she was soon found fit for trial, which kicked off in early March 1946. Any potential black jurors were "challenged pre-emptorily by the Commonwealth" and eliminated. An all-white jury of eight women and four men would decide the maid's fate.

In a last-minute decision, defense attorney Alexander decided not to seek a sanity hearing. And his defense would simply be a humane appeal for mercy for a young woman who was emotionally unstable and had probably been pushed into the crime by a more cunning and controlling mind—namely Kelly.

In his opening statement Alexander told the jury, "We will not attempt to exculpate Corrine in this shocking killing, and will not try to show that she did not do it. We will not ask you to discharge her from responsibility. Instead, we will ask you to bring in a proper safe and intelligent verdict under which she will be placed in an institution for life." He said he would also seek to prove that Sykes was under the influence of Jayce Kelly "who sent this girl out to rob."

Sykes' confession was put into evidence for the jury but not read at the trial. She reportedly admitted seeking the job with robbery in mind. Testifying in her own defense, Sykes claimed Kelly had threatened to kill her and her mother unless she robbed the house. She said Kelly waited outside in his car while she committed the robbery.

At no time during her testimony did Sykes actually admit to the murder or describe details of the slaying. When these subjects were broached, she responded either with silence or by becoming emotional. Some of the toughest questions for the maid came from the judge.

An emotional climax during the trial occurred when Assistant District Attorney Ephraim Lipschutz loudly demanded "Why did you kill Mrs. Wodlinger?" Sykes began to sob loudly. A sister sitting in the courtroom cried out, "Oh girl, tell the truth." Sykes cried even louder and then collapsed.

"Jayce" Kelly was called by the prosecution. He freely admitted he was a bootlegger, but indignantly denied any knowledge of the crime or making any threats against Sykes or her mother.

Alexander's effort to save Sykes from the electric chair was centered on testimony showing she had low intelligence and was emotionally immature. A school psychologist said testing at age 13 showed Sykes had an IQ of 63: the mental age of a child of seven years, nine months. She was stuck in the first grade until she was nine years old. At some point, her teachers felt she needed special institutional care, but there was no place to send her. Later she got into trouble for fighting and stealing and was sent to a disciplinary school.

State-appointed psychiatrist A.M. Ornsteen found Sykes to be a "constitutional psychopathic inferior." Judge Carroll asked, "Are there many constitutional inferiors walking around?" "Yes," said the psychiatrist, "and if they were all in institutions there would be scarcely anyone left on the assembly lines in industry."

In his closing argument Alexander told jurors, "She was a juvenile delinquent in 1937.... She was thrown out into the world and eight years later this happened. Should she be given the most extreme penalty known to mankind because in 1937 there was no place to send Corrine Sykes?"

"Despite the terrible features of the crime, shocking as they are, if our only penalty is to strap that child in the electric chair, turn on the current and snuff out her life, we have not advanced very far from the Dark Ages," the lawyer pleaded.

Prosecutor Lipschutz declared, "This girl lured her victim by fake references, with murder and robbery in her heart, and then slew her without mercy, leaving a motherless young daughter. If she were able to do such cunning and terrible things with a moronic mind, then heaven forbid that she could have been endowed with more intellect.... The law says when the crime is heinous, atrocious and vicious there is but one adequate punishment and that is death."

The jury returned after five hours with a verdict of first-degree murder with a recommendation of death. Sykes showed no emotion as the verdict was delivered, but collapsed when being escorted from the courtroom. Two months later Kelly was quickly convicted and sentenced to five years in prison.

Alexander feverishly filed appeals for a new trial. One line of appeal was Judge Carroll's alleged bias toward the defense. Arguing to the Pennsylvania Supreme Court, Alexander said his closing pleas to the jury "were offset if not destroyed by constant interruptions by the court."

Alexander's major hope for a new trial was his contention that he didn't know until the end of the trial that Kelly had burned the furpiece stolen from the house. He said this fact might have persuaded the jury that Kelly was deeply involved in the robbery and had probably planned it. "I think if the jury had had that evidence, it would have spared the girl's life on the grounds that Kelly was the moving factor in her taking the job with the deliberate intention to rob."

Interviewed by the press in her "immaculate" North Philadelphia home, Sykes' widowed mother, Almena, said she firmly believed her daughter was innocent. She said Corrine loved animals and was always bringing home stray cats and dogs. "But I guess she's kind of a dummy. She met up with this Jayce and she gave him everything she had. Now he's left her in this awful trouble. He's so smart. I think he's behind all this."

When all state appeals had been exhausted, Alexander filed with the U.S. Supreme Court. Twice the high court rejected those appeals. The State Board of Pardons turned down a plea for clemency. Governor Edward Martin refused to commute the sentence to life and rejected a last-minute stay.

In his pleas to the governor, Alexander pointed to the school recommendation in 1938 that she be placed in an institution. "Corrine was never placed in an institution. She was colored. There was no place for her. . . . It is therefore not the feebleminded, maladjusted Corrine Sykes who is responsible for the crime. It is I. It is you. It is all of us. It is the public, who refused to take upon ourselves the obligation which is ours to forestall such a tragedy in its incipiency."

The justice system moved swiftly in those days. On Oct. 14, 1946, just 19 months after her court conviction, Sykes was executed in Pennsylvania's electric chair at Rockview Penitentiary near Bellefonte. The 22-year-old woman was calm throughout the procedure.

More than 3,000 attended Sykes' funeral in North Philadelphia. Her mother's home was filled with friends and strangers offering their sympathy.

The execution of women has been rare in America. Fewer than 50 females have paid for crimes with their lives since the founding of the nation. Pennsylvania and New York have the highest number of female executions. Sykes became the 11th woman executed in Pennsylvania since 1781 and only the second to die in the state's electric chair. The first, "Iron" Irene Schroder, was executed in 1931 for the murder of a state trooper. Two women sentenced to death in connection with the infamous "Arsenic Ring" had their sentences commuted to life, but Sykes was not so lucky.

Rumors and legends grew up. Many believed that Jayce Kelly was protected by police because "he knew too much about their activities." It was rumored that the coroner believed a small woman like Sykes could not have inflicted such severe wounds on the larger victim.

Under the headline "Ghost of Corrine Sykes Walks Streets of City," the Tribune reported in 1950 how "a report swept the city" that a radio station announced that a white man had confessed to the crime. Later rumors alleged that "a man on his deathbed" had admitted the murder. The man's statement appeared in a newspaper "in very small type." The Tribune said it could not verify any of these reports. Raymond Pace Alexander called the rumors "silly." The newspaper ended the story on a melodramatic note: "It would seem that like the ghost of Hamlet's father, Corrine Sykes' wraith must walk the earth till all those connected with her tragic story have passed from the scene."

Sixteen-year-old Seymour Levin's crime shocked the city in 1949.

CHAPTER 9

He Belittled My Chemistry Set
Seymour Levin

In 1949 Philadelphians could still be shocked beyond words by the brutal sexual murder of one child by another child. And that is why everyone who was old enough to read a newspaper in 1949 still remembers the name *Seymour Levin.*

Sixteen-year-old Seymour seemed to be the first of a frightening new breed: a strange, vaguely troubled kid from a decent middle-class family who commits an act of senseless brutality with scant awareness of doing wrong.

The story began to unfold on Sunday morning January 9, 1949, when Donald Cohen, 21, found bloodstained clothes scattered about the backyard of his Wynnefield house and decided to call police. Officers Carmen Santaniello and Sgt. Cecil Bailey responded. In minutes they found the body of a young boy behind the garage of Cohen's next-door neighbor, Morris Levin. It didn't take a Sherlock Holmes to follow a bloody trail and some drag marks to the rear door of the Levin house.

Confronted by a body in his backyard, bloodstains on his clothes and bloodstains throughout the house and with two parents in a state of shock, the short, nerdy Seymour broke down in tears. At first he denied any knowledge of the blood or the body. But when Morris Levin shook and slapped his son and demanded the truth, the lad sobbed, "I guess I'll get the electric chair for this."

The boy in the yard—wearing only jockey shorts and covered by his coat—was 12-year-old Ellis Simons who lived several miles from the Levin house, in West Philly. His frantic parents had reported Ellis missing the prior evening. The family brought photos of the boy to The Inquirer, which police used to make a tentative identification.

The gruesome details of the murder were the source of morbid fascination for the press and public. Levin had used both a large kitchen knife and a scissors to slash and stab his victim more than 50 times. One knife thrust entered the heart, but Seymour continued to attack the dead corpse. "There was not a drop of blood left in the boy's body," said Superintendent of Detectives George F. Richardson; "it is one of the worst cases I have come in contact with in my many years in the police business." Coroner J. Allan Bertolet said, "The boy was beaten and slashed from head to foot. No part of the face, body or limbs was spared. It was the attack of a maniac."

After the slaying, Seymour tied a rope to the boy's hands and legs and dragged the body from the second-floor bathroom, down the stairs, into the kitchen, through a rear door and across the yard to a narrow space behind the Levins' detached garage. The trail showed that Seymour first dragged the body toward a large trash barrel in his neighbor's yard, but apparently decided he couldn't lift it over a hedge separating the two properties.

Later, after a not-too-thorough attempt to clean up the house, Seymour wrapped the boy's bloody clothes in newspaper and tossed the bundle from a window. Finally, he picked up his eight-year-old brother, Arnold, from their grandparents' house. His parents arrived home from their business in Toms River, N.J., about midnight. They noticed at least part of the mess and were disturbed enough to awaken Seymour for an explanation. He told his parents his chemistry set had exploded, and they accepted the explanation.

Hauled off by police for questioning, Seymour began to tell his story. He said that he met Ellis a short distance from his home, at City Avenue and 54th Street where he had gone to buy a newspaper. They struck up a conversation. Seymour invited Ellis home to see his chemistry set, and the younger boy agreed.

Seymour told detectives he took Ellis to the bathroom to show him the chemistry set. But, declared the murder suspect, the boy belittled the chemistry set, declaring that it was "cheap."

"This made me mad, and I told him to leave the house. When I said that, I saw that he had a small knife in his hand. We started to fight. We had a struggle in the bathroom." And that was all Seymour could remember. Everything that followed, he said, was a blank. There were obvious holes and lies in Levin's story, but he never wavered from his "blackout" explanation.

It was soon learned that neighbors had often complained of Seymour's behavior. He had bullied, struck and annoyed smaller kids. His parents usually took Seymour's side when complaints were voiced. More important, 18 months before the slaying, Levin was placed on probation by juvenile court. The charge was "kidnapping." What actually happened was not so dramatic. Seymour took a small boy for a ride on his bicycle, disappearing for about 50 minutes. The child's parents thought their boy was lost or kidnapped, and the incident brought police to the scene. The "kidnapping" and the previous complaints resulted in a court hearing, a psychiatric evaluation and probation.

It was also learned that Seymour had discipline and academic problems in public school. His intelligence was average, but he failed seventh grade. Things improved when his parents enrolled him in the private Oak Lane Country Day School.

Morris Levin owned a business—variously described as a dry goods or department store—in Toms River, N.J. The family lived in a spacious, single Tudor-style house at 2447 N. 56th Street, a pleasant, leafy block just behind Saint Joseph's College. It was one of the city's best residential neighborhoods.

In the days following, "10,000 curious persons" descended on the quiet block to gape. A balloon seller moved from City Avenue to 56th Street to take advantage of the crowds. Ellis Simons' funeral also drew a crowd; some 700 people who could not get inside Reisman's Funeral Chapel at 11th and Pine stood on the sidewalk.

Why Seymour lied about meeting Ellis at the newsstand is a mystery. It didn't take police long to learn that the pair had met that Saturday afternoon at a Center City movie theater. Police found ticket stubs in both boys' clothing.

Often on Saturdays, Seymour went with his parents to the store in Toms River, but on January 8, he had to make one of his regular reports to Juvenile Court on the Benjamin Franklin Parkway. It had been a good meeting. Seymour was told he was doing well and his probation would soon be over.

Because it snowed on New Year's Day, the Mummers Parade was held that Saturday. When he left court, Seymour watched the parade and snapped photos. About 2 p.m. he entered the Pix Theater at 19th and Market to watch "A Night at the Opera" with the Marx Brothers and "San Francisco" with Clark Gable. Somehow, the two boys met inside the theater and left together. Both had to take the Market-Frankford Elevated train home, and Seymour convinced Ellis to come to his house to see his chemistry set.

What happened in the house was never made clear. At Levin's sentencing a written statement by a panel of three judges declared: "It will serve no useful purpose to recite the sordid and revolting details of the murder. . . . [Levin] enticed into his home a stranger to him and there committed upon the child an act of perverted sexual lust, which an examination of the physical remains of the child incontrovertibly established."

The panel's statement ponders "why venting his lust on the victim, the defendant then proceeded to kill him . . . defendant's unnatural passion had been satisfied, the heat of sexual emotion was spent. . . . The fairly proven circumstances of this tragedy point preponderately to the conclusion that it was motivated by fear that his unfortunate victim would expose the degrading treatment to which he had been subjected."

After he was arrested for the crime, Seymour was housed in the hospital unit at the old Moyamensing Prison in South Philly. Word filtered out about his polite, quiet behavior in jail; and reporters watched him closely during several brief court appearances.

Seeing Seymour in the flesh, reporters had to agree with defense attorney James Dessen that the sadistic monster could more accurately be described as "a frightened child." He seemed "dazed," and his fingernails "were bitten to the quick." He bowed his head, held his attorney's hand, wiped away tears. When his father visited the prison the pair sobbed loudly "as both rushed to the screen, each trying to touch the face and the hands of the other through the wire mesh."

The suspect's words to police, his lawyer and father demonstrated that Seymour was not fully aware of the seriousness of the crime. "When am I going home?" he asked his father from prison. He expressed fears to police that he might not realize his ambition to become a doctor. Two weeks after his arrest, Seymour celebrated his 17th birthday in prison.

His family and lawyer decided to enter a plea of guilty. The court ordered an examination by a team of three psychiatrists to help in sentencing. The appointment of an impartial panel was praised by the news media for sparing the court and public another battle of "dueling" psychiatrists, already a common spectacle in insanity defense cases.

The psychiatrists' report declared that Seymour was neither "psychotic nor feebleminded and could distinguish between right and wrong." The experts declared, "We believe the alleged crime was motivated by strong sadistic homosexual impulses culminating in murder."

"For want of a better term," the psychiatrists labeled Seymour "a constitutional psychopathic inferior." Newspapers would soon devote many stories to these abnormal kids, often rendering the diagnosis as "CPI."

It was a thoughtful report, admitting that there was professional controversy about the term CPI, that it was little understood and hard to diagnosis. The condition, the panel said, was characterized by emotional instability, an inability to exercise self-control, impulsive behavior and disregard of ethical and moral considerations.

The report was clear that not all homosexuals were psychopaths: "The behavior of a constitutional psychopathic inferior seems to represent an attempt to unconsciously compensate, often by anti-social behavior, for strong inferiority reactions inculcated during childhood."

This description meshed well with comments to the press by the headmaster of Levin's school. John H. Niemeyer said the boy suffered from low self-esteem which he masked by showing-off to younger kids. "When Seymour arrived at Oak Lane three years ago," said Niemeyer, "he was a mess—apparently broken in spirit and suffering from a terrible inferiority complex. . . . He felt he was 'no good' and 'dumb.' But then in the first year, he regained his confidence and seemed willing to accept responsibility." He said Seymour did particularly well in chemistry and science. And the headmaster, like other adults, commented that the teen-ager seemed "very polite, almost too polite."

On March 17—a little more than two months after the murder—Seymour stood before Judges James G. Gordon, Eugene V. Alessandroni and Gerald F. Flood for sentencing. All 250 seats in the City Hall courtroom were filled. A curious crowd in the hall peered inside each time the courtroom door opened.

"Seymour Levin whispered 'I'm scared' and trembled violently today as he heard himself doomed to life imprisonment," wrote the Evening Bulletin. "He looked lonely and bewildered—just a kid in long pants—who seemed to have shrunk even smaller than his normal short stature."

Judge Gordon read a long and harsh statement meant primarily to justify the judges' decision to impose a life sentence rather than capital punishment. Mostly, it was the defendant's youth that saved him from the electric chair.

In City Hall courtyard, where a sheriff's van waited to take Levin to Eastern State Penitentiary to serve his life sentence, a crowd of 200 gathered. Seymour shrank back at the sight and told a deputy sheriff, "I'm afraid they'll hurt me." He was assured there was nothing to fear. And that was the public's last glance at Seymour Levin.

There was a spate of newspaper editorials, mostly empty rhetoric, about the need to identify and segregate dangerous child psychopaths. There was a neighborhood meeting in Wynnefield on "problem children" which drew 200.

The press had made a big deal about the numerous crime magazines and crime-related comic books found in Seymour's bedroom. This spurred regional American Legion officials to launch a campaign to ban "comic books that glorify crime."

For his own protection, the vulnerable 17-year-old youth was kept in near-isolation at America's first penitentiary. After 18 months, he was transferred to Graterford. In 1970, he was sent to Rockview in Centre County and three years later was transferred again to Muncy.

In 1962, Levin filed his first request for a pardon and was quickly rejected. It would become an annual ritual. The inmate was often represented by lawyer Morton Witkin, a passionate advocate. Witkin would reel off Seymour's accomplishments. He had become a trusty, had accumulated 180 credits through Penn State University correspondence courses and was an assistant to the visiting Jewish chaplain. "No man in Graterford has ever beaten or ever will beat the record for application to education of Seymour Levin," declared Witkin. "What more does the Commonwealth want? Do they want Seymour Levin to die in prison?"

In an emotional appeal to the board of pardons in 1972, Witkin declared "He has more college credits than I have hair. . . . He has reached the pinnacle of rehabilitation." Witkin even threatened a court challenge, charging that every Constitutional right of due process was violated when Levin's house was searched without a warrant, and in the manner the boy was questioned and his statements taken.

In 1975, the pardons board recommended that Levin's sentence be limited to 28 years. He was sent to a halfway house in Pittsburgh, where he worked at a thrift shop operated by a veterans' group and where he kept his record clean for 15 months. Finally, in June 1977, Levin was released on parole. He was 45.

The father of victim Ellis Simons was enraged by Levin's parole.

Interviewed via telephone before his release, Levin told an Inquirer reporter, "As I said in the many appeals I made to the pardons board, I committed a horrible crime and nothing can change that fact. But I have truly repented and will continue to repent for the rest of my life." He went to New Jersey to live near his father. He's well into his 60s, but for Philadelphians the name Seymour Levin instantly recalls the spooky, homicidal kid with the thick horn-rimmed glasses.

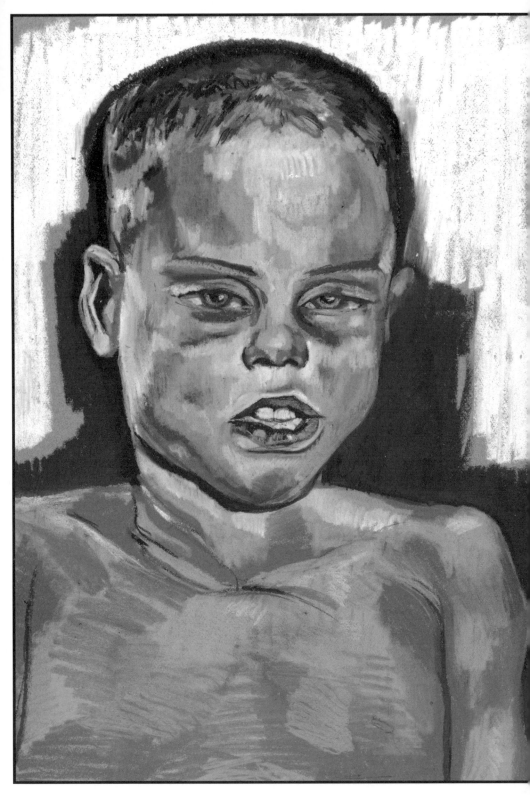

Countless copies of this post-mortem photo of the unknown
Boy in the Box flooded the city in the late 1950s.

CHAPTER 10

Bless This Unknown Boy
The Boy in the Box

It's not journalistic hyperbole to speculate that thousands of Philadelphians in their middle or later years have been "haunted" by "The Boy in the Box."

As soon as the subject is mentioned to 50-something William Fleisher, a retired FBI and U.S. Customs agent, he declares, "I was haunted by him. I must have been 13 years old when I saw his picture on the wall of an Acme supermarket. He was the first dead person I'd ever seen." Without prompting, Fleisher describes the child whose photo viewed in 1957 left a permanent imprint in his memory: "About four years old with blond hair and a bad haircut. Bruises on his forehead."

Haunted or not, countless thousands can conjure in their mind's eye the same sad, post-mortem photograph. The disturbing image of the little boy seemed to be everywhere in the Delaware Valley in 1957: in newspapers, the walls of businesses, government offices, every state liquor store. The death photo even arrived in the mail along with monthly bills to 400,000 customers of the Philadelphia Gas Works.

Among those admittedly haunted by the boy is local author Seymour Shubin, who received a complete set of police autopsy photos and pondered the mystery of the unidentified boy for 32 years. After several false starts, he penned a novel based on the boy and the unusual man most obsessed with giving the boy a name.

Remington Bristow, retired investigator of the Philadelphia Medical Examiner's Office, died in 1993. His heirs probably inherited several filing cabinets filled with documents accumulated during a relentless and fruitless 36-year quest to put a name on the boy in the box. The story of the unidentified boy is also the story of Rem Bristow.

The tale begins on February 25, 1957, when a 26-year-old La Salle College student parked his car on secluded, unpaved Susquehanna Road, in the Fox Chase section of the city's Far Northeast and walked into a thickly wooded lot.

The press would report that the man saw a rabbit, stopped and decided to follow it. Police learned that he was in the habit of sneaking through the woods to spy on the bad girls at the Good Shepherd Home. The forbidding stone building on the edge of Pennypack Park now houses the Catholic social services agency known as CORA. It was then a diocesan-run residence for "wayward girls."

In the thicket, the young man found a large cardboard box lying on its side with one end opened. Inside was the body of a little boy. Probably afraid to admit why he was in the thicket, the man did nothing. The following day, he confessed to a priest who advised calling police. He reported the macabre discovery and that same day the Evening Bulletin had the story on its front page: "Body of Boy Found in Box in Fox Chase. Victim 4 to 6, Appears to Have Been Bruised."

City Medical Examiner Dr. Joseph Spelman ruled the death stemmed from multiple head injuries, but he couldn't be sure of the cause. Despite the uncertainty, police handled it as a homicide. Bristow feels this was the first big mistake. His theory, repeated a thousand times over the years, was that the death was either natural or, more likely, accidental. "I've seen too many homicides not to know what they look like. The body was washed. He had a fresh haircut. His nails were clipped. He was laid out for burial. They did everything but call the funeral director."

Bristow believed that those who left the body would have stepped forward at some point. "But because it was labeled a homicide it scared them off."

Police were sure it would be a matter of hours or days before the little boy was identified. Occasionally, a drifter, a total stranger to the area, died in the city and his or her identity was never established. But it was rare. And never in city history had a child remained unidentified. Someone must recognize him and soon come forward with a positive ID. Immediately detectives were inundated with leads. In those early days, it seemed that the case was solved a dozen times. The press covered every hot new development.

Right off the bat, six Camden residents trooped into the city morgue at 13th and Wood and identified the body as the child of an itinerant roofer, Charles Speece. He had lived in Camden for about a month with his young son; they recognized the boy. Speece had left his wife in Lancaster and taken the boy. The mother hurried to the morgue. There was no doubt in her mind: this child wasn't her son. When Speece learned police had put out a bulletin for his arrest, he returned to Philadelphia with his son.

A young Marine—one of 18 children—arrived at the morgue. He was sure the child was a brother. His family had moved to California, but the clan was soon located on the West Coast. All the kids were accounted for.

A hot theory was that the Fox Chase boy was Stephen Damman, a child kidnapped outside of a Long Island, N.Y., supermarket in 1955 and never seen again. Little Stephen had a small, L-shaped scar under his chin. So did the boy in the box. But it wasn't Stephen.

Clues? There were loads of clues. The cardboard box, for instance, contained a shipping label with an address. It had gone to the J.C. Penney store near 69th and Market streets in Upper Darby. The box had held a baby's bassinet, and only a dozen units had been shipped to the store. Over the years police somehow located the purchasers of all but one bassinet and cleared all the buyers. Of course, most had thrown away the box; anyone could have picked it up. Amazingly, the box was not checked for fingerprints.

A blue corduroy cap—called an Ivy League cap in those days—was found close to the box. It hadn't been there long. The manufacturer's name was stamped in the hat and led to South Philly. The woman who sold the cap actually remembered the sale because the buyer had ordered a leather strap and a buckle sewn on the back. She recalled a man in his late 20s in work clothes. Hundreds of people in the neighborhood of the hat store were questioned. No one remembered a man with the blue cap and a child.

There were clues on the boy's body, particularly three small scars—two in the groin area and one on the left ankle. Dr. Spelman believed they were "cutdowns," incisions where a transfusion has been given. This meant the boy at one time was treated by a doctor or hospital. Every physician in the area was sent a flyer, and the American Medical Association circulated a nationwide description of the boy. No dice.

The boy was naked, but covered with a thin blanket that had been cut in half. Bristow had the blanket analyzed by experts at the Philadelphia College of Textiles. They pinpointed a manufacturer. But this knowledge just didn't give any help in solving the mystery.

A clue which only added a new layer of confusion, was the medical examiner's observation that one hand and one foot showed "washerwoman effect." This is the wrinkled skin caused by immersion in water for a prolonged period of time.

Another mysterious clue emerged when an ultraviolet light was shone on the boy's left eye and it fluoresced a brilliant blue. This was an unexpected find that might indicate a special diagnostic dye had been put in the eye.

Then there was the crude fresh haircut, perhaps given after death because hair clippings were found all over the nude body. One of the many creative theories hatched by Bristow is that no one recognized the boy because in life he had very long hair. Perhaps neighbors thought he was a girl. Certain ethnic groups allowed little boys' hair to grow long and dressed them in female clothes. Later, Bristow would have an artist make sketches of the boy with long hair.

Police once floated the dubious theory that the boy died of a cerebral hemorrhage caused when someone held him to cut his hair. Chief Inspector John J. Kelly told reporters, "The position of the bruises across the forehead and one at the hairline are in the same position as a person's hand would be while holding a child tightly to give him a haircut with clippers. Whoever cut his hair might have exerted too much pressure at a weak spot in the temple causing the hemorrhage."

Kelly said the bruises on the arms and legs might be the normal bumps of an active child. "Whoever caused the boy's death probably became panicky, and while in that state of mind disposed of the body."

University of Pennsylvania forensic expert W.M. Krogman examined the body and submitted a report. He found the boy's weight and bone development showed the effects of malnutrition. At 40 inches tall and 30 pounds, he was the size of a three-year-old but was probably four. He was of northern European stock, perhaps Scandinavian, German, English or Scottish. The expert's report said the corpse was a boy who had been in "chronic ill health for about a year and who, therefore, may come from a family of lower-class or reduced socio-economic circumstances." Krogman conjectured that the boy hailed from an itinerant or migratory worker's family or was a kidnapped child with the abductors constantly on the move.

Massive sweeps of the neighborhood where the body was found were carried out by as many as 350 police at one time looking for evidence. Residents in a wide area, including nearby Montgomery County, were questioned in an extensive door-to-door canvass. Scores of people viewed the body, thinking that they knew the child's identity. They arrived from both the region and a dozen states. Publicity is the friend of investigators in cracking this type of mystery. There was considerable out-of-state media interest in the case from as far away as London. Detectives followed up every promising lead no matter how far away from home it led.

It would fill a book to recount all the interesting or promising leads that led nowhere. One is particularly fascinating: Two years after the discovery of the body, Philly cops were certain the mystery was solved with the arrest in Virginia of a couple who traveled with a carnival. Kenneth and Irene Dudley were being held in the death of a six-year-old daughter whose body they had left in the woods wrapped in an old blanket. The man had already served a nine-month sentence in a New York State prison for burying another of his children in a backyard.

It turned out that six of the couple's 10 children had died of malnutrition and neglect over the years. The wretched pair simply dumped the bodies across the nation. The bodies of two kids were weighted down and sunk in Lake Pontchartrain near New Orleans. One child's body was left by the side of a highway in West Virginia. Another was left in a sulfur mine pit near Lakeland, Fla. Yes, they had been in Pennsylvania about the time the boy was found in Fox Chase. No, he was not one of their kids.

Five months after the boy was found, with investigators growing weary and frustrated, it was decided to bury the nameless boy in Philadelphia's potter's field near Philadelphia State Hospital at Byberry. A plaster death mask of the boy's face was created. Bristow and detectives who had developed an emotional stake in the case attended a service and took up a collection to mark the grave. It is the only tombstone in the entire cemetery; other graves are marked only with tiny numbers. An inscription reads, "Heavenly Father, Bless This Unknown Boy."

Other investigators felt emotional ties to the case, but for Remington Bristow it became a lifelong obsessive search. He put up reward money from his own pocket. He spent countless hours of unpaid time double-checking old leads, pouring over birth records and developing new leads, bugging the cops, giving press interviews. His vacations were often tied in with checking leads. He followed clues and hunches to California, Oklahoma, Arizona, Texas. In desperation, he turned to a psychic.

Bristow was raised in Oregon. His father was a mortician. The son followed the family trade, opening a funeral home in California. An unusual illness forced him to leave California. He settled in his wife's hometown, Philadelphia, landing the job with the medical examiner. Bristow's responsibilities included helping to determine if a death was natural or suspicious and the identity of unknown cadavers. In 19 years, he worked with thousands of unidentified bodies. Only 24 remain unsolved; one is the boy.

Asked to explain his obsession, Bristow talks about acquiring a "respect for the dead" at an early age. Certainly a more compelling reason was the death of his only son in early childhood.

The author of this book met Bristow in 1989. Chronic ill health had forced him to retire years before. He had just lost his wife. His mood was melancholy. A heavy smoker with heart, lung and circulation problems, he was in terrible physical shape. We talked about the case on several occasions.

His tales of the psychic, an elderly North Jersey woman, Florence Sternfeld, were particularly fascinating. She had worked with several police departments, and many vouched for her help. Her technique was to hold an object associated with the case—preferably something made of metal—

and spew out any vibes and ideas she was picking up.

Bristow claimed that Florence provided the key to unlocking the mystery. And he went to his grave believing he knew where the answer could be found.

The psychic spoke of seeing a house with an old wooden porch and a nearby log cabin with a child playing in it. Bristow drove around the area looking for the scene. About a mile from where the Boy in the Box was found, Bristow spotted just such an old house with a log cabin playhouse for children behind it.

He brought Florence to Philadelphia only one time. "She wanted to see the spot where the body was found, and I showed her. Then she said 'Let's go this way.'" The psychic led Bristow to the exact house with the log cabin playhouse. "She said, 'This is where you'll find the answer,'" Bristow recalls. "That was it. She said 'Take me home.' She never deviated."

At the time of the discovery, the old farmhouse was owned by a couple who cared for foster children. They usually cared for five or six kids at a time, but sometimes as many as 25 were in residence. "They took boys and girls from the state and city for a few weeks to a few years. They had a daughter who would have been about 20 at that time. There was hearsay evidence that she was an unwed mother."

The psychic focused on the house about 1960. A short time later, the couple got out of the business and sold the property. In May 1961 the contents of the place were sold and Bristow nosed round prior to the auction. He said in the basement, he spotted a bassinet. But the couple never took in babies. Bristow said he found blankets cut in half in order to fit metal cots. They were hanging on a clothesline, and he photographed them.

Not that the place had escaped police notice in the first weeks of the investigation. A detective had visited, interviewed the daughter and one of the foster kids. There were five boys and three girls in residence at the time. Both the woman and the child told the detective they never saw a boy of the subject's age at the foster home.

Something else intrigued Bristow; there was a duck pond on the property. "A dazed or injured child could have conceivably collapsed along the perimeter of the pond, one hand and one foot in the pond. This would produce the washerwoman effect."

With the circumstantial evidence of the bassinet and cut blankets, plus duck pond theory and his faith in Florence, it is amazing that the obsessed Bristow took no action at the time and continued to run around tracking other leads. His explanation? Detectives allegedly told him to "Lay off." "They told me, 'That's a nice Catholic family doing a good job for the city.'"

Finally, in 1984, Bristow tracked down the same child who had been interviewed at the foster home in 1957. Again, he did not recall the boy found in the box but said the family did give the kids home haircuts.

Next, the retired Bristow pestered homicide detectives to interview the couple again. He found their address in Bucks County. After meeting with Bristow, two Philadelphia detectives went out and questioned the elderly man.

Bristow said, "They did a half-assed job." The man continued to deny any knowledge of the boy. He said the bassinet was given to them by a friend from Frankford, but there were no follow-up questions about why a bassinet was needed."

According to Bristow, the man was asked to take a polygraph test. He said his wife was very ill, so he couldn't travel to Philadelphia, and the detectives couldn't readily arrange a home test.

With this—14 years after his first suspicions—a retired Bristow finally called the man on the telephone and engaged in a brief conversation urging him to take a lie-detector test. "He said he would [take a polygraph] but his wife was sick. There was always some excuse. He denied knowing anything about the boy."

Bristow's pet theory was that the boy was the illegitimate child of the couple's daughter and may have lived off the property. He further speculates that the boy was going to be buried in the box, but something happened to scare off the burial party.

He submitted another written report to Philadelphia police in 1985, urging them to have another interview with the man and to locate and question the daughter. With his wife's passing and in poor health, Bristow moved to Las Vegas in 1989 to be near a brother. Together, we visited the boy's grave and looked over the old house. "My granddaughter will drive me out West," said Bristow. "I'll talk to a few people as we go out. Check out a few things."

Dancer Lillian Reis and her Nemesis, Detective Capt. Clarence Ferguson,
in his trademark porkpie hat.

CHAPTER 11

Coal, A Chorus Girl and 500 Gs
The Big Score in Pottsville

Here is a tale of cops and robbers that seems to be scripted for Hollywood, replete with unexpected twists, glamour, romance, violent death, courtroom surprises, colorful crooks and colorful cops.

In fact, actor Robert Conrad became friendly with some of those involved and talked seriously of producing a film based on the saga with television Wonder Woman, Lynda Carter, in the starring role of "Tiger Lil."

One way to begin this long-running yarn is to consider three seemingly unrelated events.

Event One: This scene takes place about 90 miles north of Philadelphia in Pottsville, Schuylkill County, in late summer of 1959. Returning from a European vacation, coal company owner John B. Rich, a man the press crowned a "Coal Baron," reports a burglary in his home. He tells police $3,500 in cash and $17,000 in jewelry are missing from his basement safe—actually a fireproof metal box.

Event Two: The Evening Bulletin's entertainment page of January 8, 1960 reports: "On Wednesday night pretty Lillian Reis, who once worked as a chorus girl at the spot, took over operation of the Celebrity Room as its owner. And with Myron Cohen on hand to headline her first show, she had a packed house." The article was accompanied by a photo of the new club owner who would soon be characterized in the press as "sultry," "sexy," and "a dark-haired beauty." Never did Reis live up to the billing of "sultry" so well as in that obviously posed publicity shot. She peers coolly over a bare shoulder with large, dark almond-shaped eyes. Long tresses of dark hair curve sensuously around her face.

Event Three: About the same time that the sexy chorus girl purchases the nightclub that once employed her, Richard Blaney, a petty criminal from Kensington finds himself behind bars on a probation violation and casting about for a way out. Not having a hacksaw handy, Blaney did the next best thing: He contacted a cop and offered to trade information for an early release.

The cop Blaney spoke with was Capt. Clarence Ferguson, head of a singular band of cocky young detectives known as Clarence Ferguson's Special Investigations Squad. Like J. Edgar Hoover, "Fergy" was a legend who lived police work 24 hours a day and refused to retire. And like Hoover, the legend was as much self-created as deserved. If Fergy didn't take reporters along on a raid or an important arrest, he was sure to call the newspapers before deadline with the details.

The information that Blaney sought to swap would generate more headlines and glory for the wily, old detective than any previous case in his 51 record-setting, action-packed years as a cop. Blaney was about to snitch on some cronies from the loosely organized "K&A Gang," including his own brother, Vincent, and lovely Lillian. For shooting off his big mouth, Blaney and his brother would both die in rather gruesome fashion.

According to Blaney, certain parties were spending like drunken sailors: buying big cars, new houses and, in the case of Lillian, a $40,000 nightclub. Blaney said there had been "a big score" up in coal country, a break-in that netted the burglars somewhere between $300,000 and $500,000.

Of course, Pottsville was out of Fergy's bailiwick. But the information seemed so promising, the old cop contacted State Police. Together they launched a quiet three-month investigation that culminated in April 1960 with the arrest of a very intriguing and diverse Gang-of-Six. Fergy told the press that back on August 7, four guys from Philly pulled off the largest burglary in Pennsylvania history. He would eventually fix the haul at $478,000. And until the day he died, Coal Baron John Rich would stick to the $3,500 figure.

According to Fergy, the lovely "chorine" (a newspaper term that died decades ago) now boss-lady of the Celebrity Room on Juniper Street south of Locust, had a male admirer by the name of Clyde L. "Bing" Miller. Bing, a wealthy chap in his 50s, was absolutely crazy about Lillian. He had made a small fortune strip mining coal and would eventually detail throwing away upward of $100,000, showering Reis with cars, furs, jewelry and generous amounts of cold cash.

Fergy said when Clyde's business failed, he told Lillian about a man he knew from business dealings who kept large sums of cash in his house in Pottsville. Fergy would label Bing the "fingerman" and Lillian the "mastermind" who recruited a crew of burglars to visit the Rich mansion on Pottsville's elite Manhantongo Street.

Those arrested, along with 30-year-old Lil and Sugar Daddy Miller were alleged burglars Vincent "Barney" Blaney, 26; Robert Poulson, 24; John Berkery, 30; and Ralph "Junior" Staino, 27. Blaney, Poulson and Berkery were

Kensington-based crooks with extensive arrest records. Staino was the manager of the Celebrity Room and Lillian's true love. A handsome, broad-shouldered tough guy, Staino went along on the Pottsville caper to protect Lillian's interests, said Ferguson.

Fergy, whose trademark was the now-extinct porkpie hat—a hat with a turned-up brim—said Berkery had recently purchased a nice suburban house in South Jersey. The boys had been buying Lincolns and Cadillacs. One had laid out $500 buying drinks for the house. Ferguson said a search of Lillian's house revealed an entire room filled with clothes and furs and an income tax form showing Lil had earned $3,100 the year before.

Soon Miller, Poulson and Vincent Blaney were talking. The way they told it, the Gang was awe-struck and euphoric when they found the cabinet overflowing with neatly wrapped, sorted bundles of bills ranging from $5s to $100s. The Gang was stuffing pillowcases when a siren went off in town, sparking momentary panic. But it had actually sounded a teen curfew warning.

The Gang returned to Staino's apartment where they tossed the cash on a bed and attempted to count the haul three times. Fergy said there had been a prior agreement on a four-way split based on an anticipated haul of $100,000 or less. He said that since Lillian had put the thing together, she got the cash in excess of a hundred grand.

Richie Blaney would recall how his brother and Poulson arrived at his house that night in a state of wild elation. Each had $25,000 and "pin money" of $1,200 in five-dollar bills. Vincent Blaney stowed his cash in Richie's oven, and they went out to celebrate. Baby-faced John Berkery, labeled the head burglar, seemed to have taken a larger cut, estimated by the investigators at $100,000. "Fingerman" Bing Miller's cut was put at $7,000. The whole crew was hauled up to Pottsville and booked on burglary and larceny charges; all made bail and were soon back in Philly.

The IRS assigned an agent to the case while the Coal Baron insisted the cops were crazy: only $3,500 was missing and some jewelry. Rich was a Horatio Alger figure who had arrived penniless in the coal regions as a 14-year-old immigrant named Giovanni Battista Recchione. He worked as a breaker boy, learned to blast tunnels, became a tunnel contractor and eventually became the largest mine operator in the region. At the time of the burglary, the 66-year-old distinguished grandfather had interests in many businesses, including banking.

The early profiles of Lillian Reis portrayed her as "a stunning brunette" with a "brash manner" who danced her way from the "rough, teeming shabby Hell's Kitchen district of New York City to become a nationally known nightclub queen." She had arrived in Philadelphia about 1950, leading the chorus line at the Latin Casino. She became a hostess at the Bon Bon Supper Club. She was known for her "throaty laugh" and a favorite expression used with customers: "Drink it up, boys." The motto appeared on Celebrity Room matchbook covers. Reis had two bad marriages and was raising two young daughters.

"It's preposterous and it's so unfair," she complained to a Bulletin reporter, of the burglary charge. "Do you think I would get myself into anything like this? Money! If I really wanted just money, I could go out today and marry one of the many men with money who wants to marry me."

The initial spate of stories on Lil and the Pottsville Heist was merely the prelude for what would develop into one of Philadelphia's longest-running, most-reported crime stories of the 20th century.

Soon, the Celebrity Room was in trouble for minor violation of State Liquor Control Board regulations, and Lillian and Junior Staino got in trouble in Atlantic City for an alleged assault on a young woman. These minor distractions were followed up quickly with major developments.

While Richie Blaney was the first to snitch, Vincent Blaney and Poulson were also talking in hopes of cutting some kind of deal. In early August 1960 Poulson was beaten to a pulp, stabbed, shot in the back and dumped in the parking lot of Our Lady of Lourdes Hospital in Camden. He told a cockamamie story of a group of unknown men piling out of a car and attacking him while he waited at a South Jersey bus stop. The victim said he hailed a passing car which dropped him at the hospital. Fergy said Berkery was the prime suspect. Charges filed against Berkery were later dropped. The near-death experience convinced Poulson to clam up. Forever.

At the same time, Vincent Blaney was missing. The cops were frantically searching vacant houses and empty lots. Fergy expressed fears that "Barney" would turn up dead. And when a badly decomposed body surfaced in the ocean off Margate, N.J., Ferguson said he was "99 percent sure" it was Barney Blaney, although not even the sex of the corpse was clear. A heavy padlocked chain was wrapped around the head and torso. A 27-pound weight was attached to the chain. There was a bullet hole in the base of the skull. But not enough weight had been used. Gases in the decomposing body forced it to the surface. Two weeks later, FBI experts using dental charts provided a positive ID of the pitiful remains of Vincent "Barney" Blaney.

Six months later a weird episode commenced when shore-area burglar Robert Russell told police he had witnessed the murder of Blaney in a shore boatyard. He was full of details and names, including Berkery and Lillian, declaring that Lil laughed lustily as Blaney was blown away. The

Atlantic County prosecutor swallowed Russell's tale in one gulp. A grand jury indicted Lil, Berkery and a third man for murder. But a few months later it became clear that Russell was none too stable. And soon he would confess that the whole story was a big hoax.

March 1961 saw several events. The first trial commenced in Pottsville, for Poulson. The State Liquor Control Board notified Lil it intended to lift her license. And the Celebrity Room itself was hit by burglars who made off with $7,000 from the club's safe and several bottles of champagne. Lil said she had no insurance. The next month federal tax agents briefly padlocked the club for nonpayment of taxes.

Poulson (who repudiated his confession) was convicted. Staino and Berkery were tried jointly in May and were convicted. Lillian sobbed in sympathy for boyfriend Junior Staino.

The star witness against the Gang was now Richie Blaney. While Richie wasn't along for the heist, he said he had heard all the details from the burglars. Richie ruefully admitted that he wished he had been along for the big score. Because of the brutal death of his brother, the stout, balding crook was determined to convict the crew. In fact, Richie had become a sort of Ferguson groupie. He often rode with the colorful cop and took to wearing a Fergy-style porkpie hat.

In April 1961, Blaney said someone planted furs stolen from the home of the president judge of Common Pleas Court in the truck of his Oldsmobile. A furious Fergy declared it an attempted frame-up. Richie was a Runyonesque rogue with a quick wit. Some of the most amusing trial testimony involved verbal sparring between the cocky crook and defense attorneys. At one point Berkery's lawyer, State Sen. Benjamin Donolow, asked Richie if he was telling the truth. "If you were interested in the truth you'd plead him [Berkery] guilty," shot back Blaney. Donolow moved for a mistrial, moaning that the "remark was so prejudicial. He has been getting away with this all through the trial." Another defense lawyer asked Richie, "Is it your wits that keep you out of jail?" His answer: "No, it's my lawyers." During this period Richie got into several scrapes with the law, though Fergy, playing the role of Family Uncle, was supposed to be watching over his star snitch.

The 27-year-old wiseguy lived with his wife and three small children in a modest rowhouse on Alma Street near the Oxford Circle. In the middle of the afternoon of July 27, 1961, Blaney got into his Oldsmobile, turned the key and, as the Daily News phrased it, "was blown into eternity."

It was a sensational assassination, believed to be the first car-bomb rubout in Philadelphia history. The Daily News devoted six pages to photos and coverage. At least three sticks of dynamite were used, sending fragments of the Oldsmobile flying onto roofs and over houses. The hood of the car was found nearly half-a-block distant on a rooftop. Blaney's body was blasted into the back seat. Amazingly his watch was still ticking. Miraculously no one else was injured, although many windows were shattered.

Blaney's wife said she knew what happened as soon as she heard the blast. There had been many telephone threats. Fergy was in California on police business when Blaney died. An Inquirer reporter who contacted the detective by phone wrote that Ferguson "was bitter almost beyond words." He said the way to deal with Richie's killers was "to blow out their brains and ask questions later." When Fergy arrived home, the Daily News described him as the "the angriest man in Philadelphia. . . . Ferguson's words flowed like molten lava." He said he wasn't surprised by the murder. He, too, had received telephoned threats. Joanne Blaney threw her arms around the old detective and tearfully pleaded, "Get them, Fergy. Get them."

More than 50 suspects were questioned. Despite their convictions, Berkery, Poulson and Staino were all free on bail while appeals were being heard. All were grilled. Donolow brought Lil, Staino and Berkery into homicide headquarters for questioning; the politician/lawyer said he didn't want Ferguson's squad getting their mitts on his clients. Fergy not only blasted the lawyer, but further charged that the trio had alibis "so pat and airtight that they must have had some knowledge that the crime was to be committed."

In September, Lil and Junior Staino announced plans to marry after "all this is over." In October all attention was focused on the courthouse in Pottsville as alleged "mastermind" Lillian was tried for the Rich burglary. The case focused on her purchase of the nightclub and the source of that cash, which led to some fascinating testimony.

The defense painted a picture of Lil as a thrifty gal and a great saver who shunned banks. Estranged husband Michael Corabi told the jury that well before the Pottsville robbery, he was sitting at home watching TV when Lil came up from the basement with a hatbox and asked for help counting her savings. The box was filled with $50 and $100 bills. They counted out $29,950. And the chorus girl's stepfather, Sidney Reiskin, a jeweler from New York, testified that Lil kept $15,000 in an old valise in his basement; all pre-Pottsville cash.

But the most engaging testimony came from Sugar Daddy Bing Miller, a man many people in the packed courtroom knew. The paunchy engineer had once been an outstanding Bucknell College football player. Afterward, he built a lucrative business in strip-mining and leasing coal mining equipment.

Bing said he first laid eyes on Lil as a Celebrity Room patron in December 1953 and went ga-ga. From 1954 through 1956 Bing was flying into Philly every Tuesday night to see Lil at the club. On Wednesdays they stayed together in a hotel from 1 to 3 p.m. "It was a regular diet," said Miller, who also had a wife at home.

Bing's generosity was boundless. He paid Lillian's monthly mortgage. He threw an $1,100 birthday party for his gal. He bought her three new cars, $15,000 in diamond jewelry, $10,000 in furs. He paid for summer vacations in Atlantic City for Lillian and her kids. He paid Lil's housemaid. He said he bought her a TV, washer-dryer, refrigerator, garbage disposal. There were also many cash gifts and loans. Engaging testimony came from a furrier who said he provided Lil with inflated bills for her minks. Miller wrote the checks and the chorus girl kept the difference. A lot of the jewelry was purchased from Lillian's stepfather in New York.

Bing appeared as a prosecution witness trying to cut himself a deal, but all this titillating testimony was providing Reis with a splendid explanation of how she had accumulated the cash to buy a nightclub. And the man who sold Lil the Celebrity Room recalled her saying "God bless Bing," as she handed over a $25,000 cash deposit on the club.

Lil did not testify. Leering reporters noted she wore a different outfit each day and the scribes provided daily fashion updates. She was "clad in an olive dress with matching pumps and accessories" during closing arguments. It was said that male jurors had a difficult time taking their eyes off the attractive defendant.

The long trial was a hard-fought duel between Lil's fiery lawyer John E. Lavelle who went on to a judgeship, and dedicated Schuylkill County Assistant DA Calvin J. Friedberg, credited with displaying real courage for his relentless attack on the veracity of Coal Baron Rich. He warned the jury against "obeisance to a powerful man," adding that just because Rich is the second largest employer in the county "that doesn't make him the second most honest person in the county."

After two days of deliberations, the jury was declared deadlocked. It was nearly a 50-50 split. Those voting for acquittal said the link between the burglary and Lillian had not been clearly proved.

The year 1962 is remembered as the golden age of The Twist, and Lillian was soon crowned the local "Queen of the Twist." Strange as it may seem, Diamond Lil got in trouble for twisting in Conshohocken, Ephrata and Atlantic City. She did seem to be the target of a harassment campaign by cops, City Hall and the State Liquor Control Board. There was a constant flow of undercover cops into the Celebrity Room, plus accusations that Lil employed "B-girls" who solicited drinks, and charges of "undesirable" employees and patrons. There were full-scale raids. Members of both "Capt. Clarence Ferguson's Squad" and "Inspector Frank Rizzo's Squad" were taking an active interest in Lil's nightclub operations.

In February 1964, a cop said he tried to give a traffic ticket to Junior Staino, which led to a donnybrook that started outside and spilled inside Lillian's South Philadelphia home. It ended with three injured cops, Staino wearing a "Hahnemann Homburg" (a head swathed in bandages), and assault charges against Staino and Lil—who allegedly jumped on a cop's back. She managed to get out of most scrapes with the able assistance of a new lawyer, the brash, charming Robert "Bobby" Simone.

At one point, Mayor James H.J. Tate declared Lillian Reis and her nightclub were "giving the city a black eye." Lil had a different view: when a judge closed the Celebrity Room, she told reporters, "This is Philadelphia's loss. This is the last decent place a man can take his family."

The second Reis trial was held in Pottsville in April 1964. Simone led the defense, but the rest of the cast was pretty much the same. Dogged Cal Friedberg would prosecute again. This time the ex-chorine dressed down and took the witness stand for the first time, providing, said The Inquirer, "a bristling exchange (with Friedberg) that will not soon be forgotten in Schuylkill County Court." The jury deliberated more than seven hours and returned with a verdict of guilty. Lil wept. Fergy gave himself a verbal pat on the back.

The Queen of the Twist was released on bail while Simone appealed. Three years later the conviction was overturned, setting the stage for a third trial. Staino, Berkery and Bing Miller, all of whom had spent some time in prison, got their convictions tossed out, too. The reversals came about because federal courts struck down the principle that standing mute when being questioned about incriminating evidence is "a tacit admission" of a crime. In early 1970, a story that had stretched over a decade ended when Schuylkill County authorities, citing a variety of reasons, including costs, decided to drop all charges against Lil, Miller, Berkery and Staino. Everyone was innocent and Fergy fumed.

Simone not only rid Reis of the decade-long legal nightmare, the canny attorney also won a libel suit for Lillian and her daughters against Curtis Publishing Company. A jury found that a 1964 Saturday Evening Post cover story entitled "They Call Me Tiger Lil" not only "blackened" Lillian's reputation but moreover incorporated a lot of biographical information stolen directly from an autobiography the ex-chorine had been writing. It awarded Lil and the kids a whopping $1.8 million. Lillian shed tears of joy. Fergy called the libel verdict "a joke." A panel of judges found it excessive and pared down the figure to less than $500,000.

The "Big Pottsville Heist" was laid to rest, but the well-known cast of players continued to make news. Reis was arrested in Miami and sentenced to two years in prison for possession of a single marijuana cigarette. It took many years to finalize a divorce from her second husband, but in 1978 she was free to marry Staino.

Ferguson died at age 75 in November 1971. No other Philadelphia cop had ever received more awards, arrested more bad guys or had such an intimate knowledge of the local underworld. Even Lillian Reis had a few nice words for Fergy.

John Carlyle Berkery attained near-legendary status as a witty, wily and charismatic career criminal who managed to avoid any lengthy jail-time despite a reported 36 arrests. In the early 1980s Berkery become one of 38 defendants indicted on charges of dealing in multimillion dollar quantities of P-2-P, the chemical used to make methamphetamine or speed. Berkery and mobster Raymond "Long John" Mortorano disappeared. Mortorano was soon found, but it took more than five years to nab the elusive Berkery.

Not that investigators didn't know where to find their prey: Berkery sent letters from Ireland to Federal Prosecutor Louis R. Pichini, saying he missed TastyKakes and wanted to cut a deal. He humorously lamented the damp discomforts of Eire. "Here I am with an umbrella and hot-water bottle. I've been gone the better part of three years, the equivalent of a five-year sentence, at my own expense." Berkery said if Pichini were in his shoes, he would have done the same thing, "but at least you'd be in sunny Italy. . . . What are we proving? I'm sure the crime rate didn't go down since I left. Gimme a break, Mr. P. I'm starting to feel like the poor man's Robert Vesco."

It's hard to believe Berkery was truly miserable in Ireland. He had acquired a stunning girlfriend and traveled a lot, even making several trips to the United States using an alias. In June 1987, the debonair rogue was nabbed along with a brother and his "raven-haired" sweetheart in a Mercedes-Benz near Newark Airport. Berkery was allegedly involved in another big P-2-P deal.

He was convicted of the old drug charges, sentenced to 15 years, won a new trial with an appeal that he wrote himself and then made a plea bargain that got him out of jail in the early 1990s.

References to the old K&A Gang by Daily News columnist Larry McMullin in 1993 prompted Berkery to dash off a letter to the editor. "I've got my own 'K&A Gang' now, Larry—a son who's a CPA, another who's a general manager for a national restaurant chain, a daughter who teaches school, another who works for the school board, two more daughters in grade school and a baby who might be the next heavyweight champion of the world."

At the same time that Berkery was on the lam, Staino would be linked to the organized crime family of Nicademo "Little Nicky" Scarfo and dealing in P-2-P. In the late 1980s Staino was convicted in separate trials on drug charges and racketeering. For a seven-month period, Staino hid out in a beachhouse in the Dominican Republic. When he was captured police found a diary. Staino had a Dominican girlfriend for a time, but the diary reveals a loving, thoughtful and human side of a notorious tough guy, a man with a terrible aching for the woman who had shared his life for nearly 30 years.

Examples: "Boy, do I miss Lillian. Not just for sex. For compassion, for understanding, for conversation, for above all love. . . . I didn't realize how difficult it was to hide a broken heart. . . . I die a thousand deaths each day. No one can ever know unless they've lived a life alone."

Staino was tracked down and returned. On May 3, 1989, a federal judge put him away for 33 years. Staino tried to read a statement in court pleading for leniency so he could spend his last years with Lillian, her daughters and grandchildren. He choked up and cried after a few words. His lawyer had to finish the statement. Lillian and her grandchildren wept with him.

Tough Tony Scoleri was highly intelligent and capable
but couldn't avoid trouble and tragedy.

CHAPTER 12

The Enigma of Tough Tony
Tony Scoleri

He is perhaps the most intriguingly enigmatic personality to emerge on the Philadelphia crime scene in the second half of the 20th century .

None of the clichés truly explain the puzzling life and complex soul of Anthony "Tough Tony" Scoleri. He wasn't exactly a "Man of Two Faces," or "a Jekyll and Hyde" or an "evil genius." Nor does he appear to be the consummate actor, repeatedly fooling everyone by guile into the belief that Tough Tony was at last rehabilitated and would now fulfill his obvious potential. No, he seemed to really change and then proceed to squander each second, third and fourth chance that society granted.

He would make a fascinating psychological study, but mostly what we know about Tough Tony comes in the form of scores of sensational, interesting but ultimately unsatisfying newspaper stories stretching over decades and ending in his 1980 suicide.

He was one of eight children—seven boys and a girl—from a poor South Philadelphia family. He plunged headfirst into a life of crime as a kid. At 13 he did his first stint in reform school. By age 17 his police record included aggravated assault, highway robbery, burglary, auto theft and shoplifting. In 1948, at age 19, Scoleri and three companions confessed to a spree of 22 armed stickups in a little more than two months. Their victims were small corner stores, mostly druggists and grocers, in South Philly. The total haul for all 22 heists was $2,400.

An obvious hard-core case, Scoleri was sentenced to 20 to 40 years at Eastern State Penitentiary. Within a short time the short, thoughtful felon with the thick eyeglasses sought guidance from Baptist clergyman Anthony F. Vasquez, who visited the prison each week. Scoleri had known the minister in South Philly where Vasquez was pastor of St. John the Baptist Church at 13th and Tasker streets.

The young inmate attended all of Vasquez's religious services, and over the years wrote the minister a thick stack of thoughtful, introspective and articulate letters. They told of his new religious life and his determination to change. In one letter he writes about the skepticism surrounding his rehabilitation: "There is much speculation regarding this change. I have been called everything from a poor crackpot to a first-class actor. Like a popular tune, over and over is repeated a leopard can't change his spots, he's bugs or he's putting on an act. This, even though they will concede that something definite and decisive has happened."

Years later the minister would tell reporters, "No man showed a greater change than Tony." Scolari counseled with other prisoners. He spent endless hours in religious study. He completed his high school studies.

"He was a great force there," declared the preacher. "He helped a good number of men. The man became a symbol. After a few years, guards and psychiatrists said, 'This is a miracle.'"

Indeed, he impressed all, including the parole board. After serving only six years of his 20-to-40 year sentence, Tough Tony was paroled at the end of 1955.

Upon his release, he left the Catholic Church, became a Baptist, worked in a steel cabinet manufacturing plant, studied religion and even spoke on delinquency at a national conference of penologists. A year later, he was a student at the Baptist-sponsored Alderson-Broaddus Theological Institute in Phillipi, West Virginia.

But during the summer break of 1958, the 29-year-old divinity student returned to his old turf and his old instincts. He pulled an armed stickup of a corner store in South Philly. What appeared to be a tragic but common-enough robbery-murder of storekeeper Max Gordon was to make Tony Scoleri—and his colorful companions—a source of fascination and sensational news copy for years to come.

"Thugs Slay Merchant in Wild Battle," read the Inquirer headline on Aug. 29, 1958. Gordon, 42, operated a variety store on the corner of Newkirk and Reed, near 28th Street. He also cashed checks and sold money orders, which led the stickup team to believe there was a good deal of cash on the premises. In the end, Max Gordon lost his life and Tough Tony ended up on Death Row for $18.

The robbery commenced shortly before 9 p.m. Gordon and his wife, Rose, were seated in a room behind the store. Their 16-year-old daughter and her boyfriend were watching television in the basement.

Two gunmen entered the store. When Gordon balked, he was struck on the head with a gun butt. The shopkeeper fell to the floor bleeding and $18 was taken from his pocket. The two teens, hearing the commotion, came upstairs. All four were held hostage in the back room. Gordon was given a towel to staunch his bleeding head. The two robbers ransacked the living quarters, and the leader demanded to know where the storekeeper kept his money.

Gordon led the robbers into his store, bent over a counter, lifted the lid of a cash box and came up with a .32 caliber revolver. He got off a couple of shots, wounding one of the bandits. The other gunman shot Gordon twice and the pair departed.

Max Gordon died an hour later in Philadelphia General Hospital. The fleeing bandits were pursued by a group of neighborhood kids as they made their way to a getaway car parked two blocks away. The wounded man had to be helped along. At one point, Scoleri turned and fired a warning shot at the kids. A driver was waiting. One of the nervy youngsters tossed a bottle that broke against the fleeing auto.

The robbers were Tony Scoleri and Richard "Ricky" Woods, 21, a light-skinned African-American with bleached blond hair. Waiting for them in the car was Scoleri's younger brother, Joseph Edward Scoleri, 23, known as "Eddie."

The trio headed to the apartment of Ida Iocco, 25, on Dickinson Street near 16th. The Daily News described Iocca as "a slender, olive-skinned brunette." She would be characterized as Tony Scoleri's "gun moll," Scoleri's girlfriend and the girlfriend of Ricky Woods.

Also at the apartment was a friend of Ida and the Scoleris. This attractive young woman had a name that could have been created by a Hollywood agent: Denise Devonshire. In that pre-feminist era, reporters would never fail to note that Devonshire was "shapely" or "an attractive brunette." At some point, another Scoleri brother, Dante, arrived at the apartment.

Tony asked Dante to take the severely wounded Woods to the hospital. "We'll take him down to the tracks and blow his brains out," was Dante's reply according to Iocco's later testimony. The wounded man dies in the apartment before dawn.

The next morning, Tony Scoleri coolly kept an appointment with his parole officer, betraying no sign that anything was amiss. The corpse of Ricky Woods lay in the apartment for almost two days before the Scoleris drove it to South Jersey and buried the young robber in a shallow grave. Police learned the identity of the robbers when the car—registered to Eddie Scoleri—was found abandoned in South Jersey.

Then the excitement commenced. Tony, Eddie and Ida took off on a three-week cross-country robbing and looting spree, making headlines as a team of Philadelphia's top detectives and lawmen from nine states stayed hot on their tracks.

"The nation's police departments were blanketed today with 70,000 stop-the-Scoleris circulars in the biggest Philadelphia-directed manhunt in 13 years," declared the Daily News. In addition, "another 50,000 circulars have been expressed to 7,000 police departments in all cities of more than 2,500 population coast-to-coast." It was the biggest Philly manhunt since Slick Willie Sutton and several other inmates dug out of Eastern State Penitentiary in April 1945.

The circulars worked. The brothers were nabbed by plainclothes cops in Kansas City, but not before providing many vicarious thrills to Philly newspaper readers. It was during the chase that the press pinned a new nickname on Tough Tony. He became Anthony "Mad Dog" Scoleri.

The trio's first stop was West Virginia, where Tony looked up a friend from divinity school and borrowed his car. In Toledo they kidnapped, then freed, a traveling salesman, taking his car and wallet. They spent three days in Cleveland where they robbed a grocery store. Ida went to a Cleveland beauty parlor and became a blonde. Tony, who wore thick glasses, got fitted for contact lenses but never picked them up. And Eddie dyed his hair red.

Next, they were off to Chicago where Tony and Ida took a room on the North side of town. The two brothers stuck up two Chicago drugstores, taking a load of "uppers" and "downers" along with cash.

Then came a bizarre but major development. A man dropped a badly burned woman at a Chicago hospital and quickly disappeared. The man was Tony Scoleri. The burn victim was Ida Iocco, who was initially given a 50-50 chance of survival. Exactly what had happened was a mystery. In the end, it appeared that Ida had taken an overdose of sleeping pills, fallen asleep while smoking and set her bed on fire. The flying squad of Philly detectives quickly arrived a her bedside and Ida began talking. Her information quickly led to Ricky Woods' grave in New Jersey.

The Scoleri Brothers next appeared in Springfield, Ill., where they robbed a jeweler of $6,000 in diamonds and $400 in cash. Next, they abandoned a car near Kansas City.

Two plainclothes detectives eating lunch in downtown Kansas City noticed the pair; Eddie's dyed red hair stood out. They went back to the police station, checked Wanted flyers and realized they had just seen the Scoleri Brothers. They returned to the area, searched for the pair and spotted their quarry outside a bus station.

The two lawmen approached the brothers with drawn guns. Tony reached for his weapon. When one of the Kansas City detectives fired a warning shot, both brothers surrendered. Tony would later claim he wanted to be shot and killed.

The Philly detectives zoomed to Kansas City, and Eddie immediately began talking. He admitted driving the getaway car, but maintained that

Tony had nothing to do with the Gordon robbery-murder. The brothers were returned to Philly by train under heavy guard. Ida Iocca came home under guard by plane. She was taken to Philadelphia General Hospital where surgical attempts to save her badly burned right arm failed, and it was amputated.

By September 22, the Scoleris were locked up and by mid-November Tony Scoleri was on trial in a City Hall courtroom. The judge was Vincent A. Carroll, a cantankerous, hard-nosed jurist noted for speedy justice. Declaring he "would accept no dillydallying, Judge Carroll prodded the attorneys into picking a jury of six men and six women in less than five hours," wrote the Evening Bulletin. Plenty of drama lay ahead as spectators lined up for courtroom seats. Mrs. Gordon, her daughter and the boyfriend all identified Tony Scoleri as the gunman who killed Max Gordon.

Denise Devonshire and Ida Iocca, appearing as prosecution witnesses, provided excitement and glamour. "The courtroom was in a near uproar yesterday when Assistant District Attorney Paul M. Chalfin took the wraps off his mystery witness, Miss Devonshire," wrote the Daily News.

A reporter interviewed workers at the Sheraton Hotel where Denise was staying under protective custody: "A busboy said, 'A looker like her is the kind of molls they have in the movies.'" Along with Ida and Denise, a young man named Harry Shinock had overheard the two brothers plan the robbery. "Ida had the courtroom gasping when she gave details," wrote the Daily News.

The 14-year-old kid who had chased the fleeing bandits and thrown a bottle at their car identified Tony Scoleri. A few days later the same intrepid lad was back in the news when he was arrested for a burglary.

In the middle of the trial, Tony attempted suicide in his cell at Holmesburg Prison. Using a piece of broken mirror, he slashed an arm and wrist. The bleeding suspect fought guards trying to get him out of his cell. The wound required 24 stitches.

The suicide attempt occurred about 6:30 a.m. But three hours later, the defendant was in the courtroom, stitched-up and stuporous from tranquilizing drugs. A disgusted Judge Carroll postponed the trial for a few hours but later in the afternoon testimony continued with Tony lying on a stretcher.

Tough Tony's major defense witness was his brother Eddie, who was waiting to be tried separately. The youngest Scoleri swore that the two men who shot it out with Max Gordon were Ricky Woods and a certain Joseph "Yogi" Santarpio who—coincidentally—had recently been killed in a barroom brawl.

Tony took the witness stand—while 400 crammed into the courtroom and another 400 were turned away. He admitted helping his brother get rid of Woods' body but declared he had no role in the holdup. The defendant's sister said Tony was hanging around at the restaurant where she worked that night. Rebuttal witnesses shot holes in the defense, providing convincing testimony that Yogi was working in an auto shop at the time of the Gordon robbery.

One of the last acts in the trial was the reading of Tony's extensive criminal record to the jury. Judge Carroll said this information was strictly to help the panel fix the penalty if they found Scoleri guilty.

The jury did, indeed, find that Tony was the triggerman who killed Gordon and set the penalty at death in the electric chair.

Eddie's trial was next. A defense psychiatrist asked for a delay. While Eddie was legally sane, he seemed to be on the brink of a nervous breakdown, said the shrink. No dice. The trial proceeded.

About the same time that Eddie's trial was set to start, the press latched onto a juicy morsel of news and played it to the hilt. "Scoleri Dolls' Hotel High Jinx Probed," screamed a Daily News headline.

City controller Alexander Hemphill was disturbed by the high food and beverage tab being run up by Ida Iocca, Denise Devonshire and Harry Shinock, who were in protective custody at the Sheraton and, later, the Essex hotels. The implication and real scandal was that detectives guarding the trio were living high off the hog. "Les Girls de l'Homicide," said the Daily News, were ordering filet mignon, drinking grasshoppers, martinis and vodka collins. Everybody from the police commissioner to the district attorney was caught up in the fray. In the end, it was decided that the bills were not out of line, and everyone was cleared.

In the middle of Eddie Scoleri's trial, he changed his plea to guilty. The sobbing 22-year-old told the court he would "give both his arms if it could bring Max Gordon back." He was rewarded with a life sentence. Both brothers were now in Eastern State Penitentiary, Tony on Death Row, Eddie a lifer. But this was not the end of the Scoleri Saga. There was much more to come.

In prison, Tony got into fights with other inmates and was a constant disciplinary problem. He attempted suicide again by slashing his wrists. And in January 1961 Tony and Eddie were both part of a violent escape attempt by 32 maximum security inmates which left two guards badly wounded. It required a platoon of State Police to gain control of the situation.

In the meantime, Scoleri's lawyer was filing appeals, arguing that the drug-induced stupor following Tough Tony's suicide attempt made it impossible for him to aid in his own defense. But the argument that convinced a federal appeals court to overturn his conviction and grant a new trial was the prejudicial effect on the jury of hearing Scoleri's arrest record. The U.S. Supreme Court upheld the decision.

In October 1963 the second trial of Tony Scoleri kicked off with a lengthy jury selection procedure. With one juror needed to complete the panel, Scoleri shocked everyone—except his defense attorney Michael von Moschzisker—by changing his plea to guilty.

Now a three-judge panel would hear the evidence, decide the degree of murder and set the penalty. One of the era's sharpest legal eagles, First Assistant District Attorney Richard A. Sprague, made it clear that he would urge the death penalty. Before accepting the plea, Judge Maurice W. Sporkin ensured that Tony knew that death was a possibility.

The three judges heard all the witnesses, including Max Gordon's widow and daughter, who was now married to boyfriend Jack Dinerman. The judges deliberated for 15 minutes and returned with a verdict of first-degree murder. They unanimously set the penalty at death.

Now it was lawyer von Moschzisker who was in shock. In open court, he declared that one judge, Theodore L. Reimel, had promised a life sentence. He asked Reimel to testify and wanted to withdraw the guilty plea. "I am shaking with shock," declared Sprague. "Trying to fix a judge is no different than trying to fix a jury."

A surprised Reimel said von Moschzisker had asked him a hypothetical question and in reply he said he would give a life sentence. "But the facts in this case were entirely different. . . . I must say it is most unusual for a member of the bar to make such a statement."

Von Moschzisker recounted his conversation with Reimel. He said that on the basis of that particular discussion, he had urged Scoleri to change his plea; indeed, Scoleri said his lawyer's assurance of getting life was the only reason he pleaded guilty. The judges denied von Moschzisker's motion to withdraw the guilty plea. For the second time in his life Tough Tony heard a judge condemn him to death in the electric chair.

The brouhaha and the dark shadow it cast over the judicial system forced the Pennsylvania Supreme Court to set aside the whole mess and set the stage for a third trial in September 1964.

John Rogers Carroll was Tony's new lawyer. Sprague again prosecuted. Judge Raymond Pace Alexander presided. The entire cast of characters—44 witnesses—replayed their 1958 testimony, including the widow, the daughter, the boyfriend, Ida Iocco, Denise Devonshire, the cops. Even the kid who threw the bottle told his tale again.

Tony took the stand in his own defense to say he was at his sister's restaurant during the robbery. Afterward, he dropped by Ida's apartment where Eddie arrived with the dying Ricky Woods. Yes, he helped bury the body. But, he told the jury, "Eddie is the youngest in the family. He's my baby brother. And I couldn't turn my back on him."

The jury deliberated over two days, but the result was the same: Guilty of first-degree murder. And again the jury recommended death. Three trials. Three death sentences.

By this time, Scoleri was at Graterford Prison. He was to spend a total of 14 years on Death Row, a block holding a dozen men totally isolated from the rest of the prison. The transformation of the late 1940s and early 1950s was now to repeat itself. Now the law rather than religion was the catalyst of a reborn Tough Tony Scoleri.

Scoleri was building a reputation as the state's most accomplished jailhouse lawyer. "The Dean of Death Row" was writing excellent legal briefs for himself and his fellow Death Row denizens. His abrasive personality was mellowing. He taught a totally illiterate inmate to read. He started working on a college degree through correspondence courses.

In June 1972 the U.S. Supreme Court declared the death penalty, as it was meted out, was "cruel and unusual." Five affected Graterford inmates were allowed to meet the press. Scoleri was the most talkative, declaring that what he really wanted was another trial. "It's a question of justice," he declared. True there had been three trials, but none was "fair."

Scoleri was now placed in the general prison population. Then a new, liberal Graterford warden, Robert Johnson, allowed Tony to set up a law clinic to serve the inmates. He was given a room and a staff of 10 inmates. A glowing report by United Press International said other states were studying the concept.

An even more positive story appeared in The Inquirer Sunday Magazine in 1973. It was a lengthy, warm and fuzzy piece focusing on the close bonds of friendship and mutual "growth" of convict Tony and correctional officer Edward Shaw.

During the summer of 1977, Scoleri became a bridegroom! In a jailhouse ceremony, he married a widow with grown children who came to Graterford to visit a relative. Somehow they met and fell in love.

In September 1979—21 years after his first conviction for the Gordon murder—the state parole board agreed that it was time to release its brainy, model prisoner. Now 50 and gray-haired, Tony was a classical music buff who had earned a college degree and hoped to find employment as a social worker. He was also writing a book about his life.

Less than three months after his release, Tough Tony wrote the final surprise and bizarre chapter of a strange and tragic life. He committed suicide.

He had been working as a maintenance man in an apartment complex in Fort Washington and living with his wife in a trailer in Trainer, Montgomery County. "Like a parasite, something from the Tough Tony days had crept into his new life," wrote The Inquirer. Whitemarsh Township police wanted to question him about a burglary at the apartment complex. The newspaper characterized it as "a two-bit burglary."

On Christmas Eve, police came to his trailer and searched it while the couple was away. Tony's stepson told him that the police wanted to see him. The ex-con called police and said he wanted to spend his first Christmas after 21 behind bars with his new family. Then he would voluntarily come in. Not sure where he was calling from, police had no choice but to grant the request.

The couple checked into a motel in Media, Pa., for their first and last Christmas together. They spent part of Christmas at Tony's stepson's house. They left their motel during the pre-dawn hours, stopping at a convenience store. Among the items Tony purchased were blades for a scraping tool.

With his wife driving, they arrived at their trailer. It was only then that she noticed Tony sitting in a pool of blood. He had ripped open his forearm with the blade. For a half-hour, Tony tried to convince his wife to let him die. When an ambulance finally arrived, he had lost 75 percent of his blood and suffered a heart attack. He lingered two days before dying.

His parole officer and friends tried to make sense of it. Certainly, he would have gone back to prison to await trial on the burglary charges. Maybe he just couldn't face prison bars again.

A black cop who worked in the suburbs and lived in the apartment complex had become friendly with the ex-con. They had the same sense of humor and love of classical music. He was at Tony's bedside when he died. Interviewed by The Inquirer, the cop said, "He was—what's the best way to put it? A newlywed? A clown? He was trying to cram 20 years, trying to live it all, suck it all in."

At 700 pounds, Sylvan Scolnick was Philly's heaviest and brainiest criminal.

CHAPTER 13

Huge Body, Big Brain
Sylvan Scolnick

By most measures, Sylvan Scolnick was the brainiest, most audacious, most imaginative, sophisticated, enterprising, voracious and versatile criminal in Philadelphia history.

He was certainly the fattest criminal of his era—toting around 500 to 740 blubbery pounds on a six-foot frame. To a large extent, the press was too infatuated with "Cherry Hill Fats'" immense girth to fully appreciate his enormous achievements in his chosen profession.

Scolnick was a master criminal who combined audacity and imagination with such serious dedication and thorough preparation that he managed to steal an estimated $20 million to $50 million for himself and his henchmen during a brief six-to-seven year criminal career.

In his biography, *Alias Big Cherry*, The Fat Man complained of having too much cash to handle. "It got so I was even sorry I had the frigging money," he groused. During a single week the master crook purchased three new Cadillacs and three Chryslers and gave them away as gifts. He once walked into a furrier's, picked out two matching mink coats for his wife and mother, reached into his pocket and peeled off $8,000 in front of an astonished owner.

Scolnick told of the time he and his father-in-law worked until dawn ripping out wood paneling in his den to hide excess cash. The next morning he sat admiring his handiwork; he had put back the paneling perfectly. A brother stopped by, looked around, and said, "Man, all that paneling would sure be a great place to hide money behind." As soon as the brother left, Scolnick ripped the panels out again and removed the cash.

The loot poured in from a mind-boggling variety of crime. The vast range of his unlawful enterprises, alone, makes Scolnick a world-class crook. He was most famous for his many complex bankruptcy-fraud schemes. But the list includes counterfeiting everything but money, insurance scams, mortgage scams, fleecing Las Vegas casinos, blackmail and extortion, a variety of bank fraud, loan-sharking, credit card fraud, home-improvement scams and arson. He disavowed crimes of violence, but through associates he found himself involved in a truck hijacking and a fake stickup.

A scam that failed provides a stunning example of Scolnick's bold and imaginative scheming. The idea was sparked by the fact that buying property or business always involves the transfer of one check—no matter how huge—on the day of settlement. With this in mind, Scolnick decided to buy a chain of department stores.

He set up a crony as the representative of an imaginary syndicate of investors with interests in the jewelry business. The bogus group was seeking to buy department stores selling large quantities of jewelry. Scolnick leased an expensive suite for the con man, fitted him out with a fine wardrobe, furnished a rented limousine and driver. The front man then contacted a well-established, reputable lawyer who was paid a $1,000 retainer to help in the search.

In the meantime Scolnick, who owned a print shop employing a master counterfeiter, had several blank cashier's checks from a major New York bank printed up.

It took about two months, but the lawyer—an unknowing dupe—found a business broker with a chain of stores in the Boston area for sale at $28 million. Scolnick's man was interested but insisted on an exhaustive audit of the store's books.

The plan was to make settlement on a Friday, which is normal. The store would get the check for $28 million, plus any money in its cash cages and safes. Scolnick's man would then get the keys. Over the weekend, the gang would clean out the jewelry and cash. They had plenty of time; Scolnick knew it would take three banking days for the cashier's check to clear. Scolnick invested $7,500 in the scheme, but was certain he would net more than $1 million. The Fat Man spent a full week with his front man teaching him how to handle the details of the settlement.

Alas, as was to happen often, Scolnick misjudged the intelligence of his partner in crime. The crook was told to leave no fingerprints and to make no personal phone calls from the rented apartment. Not long before the sting was to be consummated, Scolnick discovered the nitwit had thrown parties in the apartment. There were fingerprints everywhere. Worse, he made phone calls to his wife, his mother and two calls to Scolnick. The telephone company of course would have records of these calls.

Scolnick immediately closed-down the scam. He had to satisfy himself with a small profit made by passing some of the counterfeit cashier's checks.

There are a couple of images of Scolnick, who died of a heart attack in 1976, that linger in the memory. One is a photo that appeared in newspapers around the nation of the massive Scolnick being wheeled into federal court seated on a dolly used to move sacks of mail. He claimed to be too heavy and ill to walk at the time. The other enduring memory of Scolnick was his success in planning a scheme used by burglar Sidney Brooks to steal his own safe-deposit box, stuffed with $100,000, after the feds had sealed the box.

Brooks was among a host of underworld characters, racketeers and petty thieves who were friends or business associates of Scolnick. The Fat Man was the intellectual superior of his crooked cronies, and they often turned to him for advice, especially when they were in a jam. When Brooks was arrested as a burglary suspect, police found a key to a safe-deposit box on him. They quickly located and opened the box at a PSFS branch bank on Cottman Avenue in the Northeast. The IRS was notified of the huge stash and quickly impounded and sealed the box.

Released on bail, a seething Brooks sought advice from Scolnick. The Big Man mulled the matter over and came up with a plan based on the assumption that bank tellers are often sloppy with master keys to deposit boxes. They might leave the key on the top of a desk or in an unlocked drawer. Brooks had a duplicate key for his own box. But it always takes two keys to open a box, so he needed the bank's master key.

Scolnick enlisted two lackeys, Allen Rosenberg and Kenneth Paull. One was to rent boxes at the bank until he got one close to Brooks' impounded box. He was also to actively use the boxes to get bank employees used to seeing him. One day when he was at his box, a diversion would be created. The second henchman would be watching to see where the clerk left her keys. They would then switch boxes.

Brooks, who wanted to be close to his money, created the diversion on a busy day by throwing a brick through the bank's window. One of the inside men helped by leading the customers and clerks to the front of the bank. The second man took the master keys from the top of the unattended desk. He broke the seal and stole Brooks' box. However, he disobeyed the boss' instruction by placing the box under his raincoat and leaving with it. Scolnick felt the theft might have gone unnoticed for a long period if the pair had switched boxes.

Brooks was elated. Scolnick's cut was $15,000; the two henchmen split $5,000. It was an ingenious but simple ruse that worked perfectly. The plan included a patented Scolnick flourish. Brooks would sue the bank for losing his $100,000. This bit never came off because soon Brooks, Scolnick, Paull and Rosenberg would all be in deep trouble with the law and squealing on one another in efforts to cut a better deal with prosecutors.

Scolnick was born in Philadelphia into a family of modest means. He disliked school and dropped out of Northeast High School, at 8th and Lehigh Avenue, with only a half-year left until graduation. He was always overweight. One news article during his time in police custody claimed he was scarfing down 54 hamburgers "with fixings" daily. However, many of those who knew him well say he ate normal amounts and were convinced the root of his weight problem was glandular.

The Fat Man said his first crime was reporting a car stolen and putting in a false insurance claim that was paid when he was 22. He had a heart attack at age 29. He went into crime full-time after his recovery, rationalizing that he would probably die young and needed to make money for his family.

His first bankruptcy fraud was hatched in early 1959 with his father-in-law, upholsterer Morris Stein, as the front man. Scolnick's method was to set up a retail store and begin ordering merchandise by telephone on credit. He would open a bank account to prove he had cash. If the suppliers wanted a financial statement, Scolnick would gladly furnish one showing a booming business. Sometimes he would buy a small business with a long history and good credit.

He would begin setting up a sting by buying in small quantities. He would pay promptly and immediately make a larger order. He would establish credit with scores of suppliers. In the end, merchandise was arriving at the front door by the trailer-load and going out the back door just as quickly. He was selling to "legitimate" stores and buyers at 25 to 50 percent below the wholesale price. The buyers, of course, knew what was going on. Soon they were telling the con man what they wanted and where to order.

He would boldly order enormous quantities from hundreds of suppliers. The goods ranged from television sets to antifreeze to cookies. During the nine months that Morris Stein was in business he ordered goods worth $1.2 million and went bankrupt with debts of $623,775.

Scolnick always claimed these scams could not succeed without the greedy buyers. He also depended on the greed of suppliers. Credit managers might question a huge sale to an obscure outfit in Philadelphia, but sales managers, greedy for a big sale and a big commission, would overrule such qualms.

Besides capitalizing on greed, Scolnick relied on the fact that the apparatus of federal bankruptcy is geared to obtaining and dividing assets, not ferreting out fraud. Scolnick knew there was no law against keeping messy books or no books at all. The front man for the bankrupt company—Scolnick always stayed in the background—would claim he was not only a lousy businessman but was always a compulsive gambler to boot. That's how the money disappeared.

So many of these bankruptcies were occurring in the area that the feds, prompted by an astute lawyer, Meyer Maurer, started an investigation. Philadelphia Magazine learned many of the details of the operations and published a long article in May 1964, mentioning Scolnick for the first time. But it would take two more years before the master crook was charged with a crime. And most of the evidence was coming from stoolies in trouble with the law.

Scolnick was most proud of the half-dozen ways he developed to swindle big bucks from banks. Sometimes it was as simple as opening a bank account, keeping it active to look legitimate and then slipping in a phony check. Before the bad check could be returned, Scolnick would clear out the account and disappear. In yet another scam his people made scores of bad bank loans using phony identifications. Telephone numbers to verify credit references would ring at Scolnick headquarters. "You walk out of there in 20 or 30 minutes with $2,500. You can do five or six banks a day like this. . . . At one time I had 10 guys going in for loans working in teams, all over the country," boasted the master scoundrel in his biography.

At one point, Scolnick operated a second-mortgage loan office in Camden. People desperately in debt would take out a $3,000 consolidation loan with their house as collateral. But all the cash was coming from a bank, and somehow Scolnick was making close to $2,000 on each loan.

Scolnick's counterfeit operation did a brisk business in American Express Travelers Cheques and all forms of identifications. He even printed phony insurance policies that he would sell to people who couldn't easily buy fire or auto insurance. He once purchased a load of cheap paint at 55 cents a can. He replaced the labels with counterfeit DuPont Paint labels and sold the paint to contractors for $2.50 a can.

He was involved in an insurance-fraud fire set by Sidney "The Torch" Brooks in March 1965 at a home improvement firm that Scolnick was involved with on Frankford Avenue near Bridge Street. The blaze got out of control, destroyed seven buildings and did more than $600,000 in damage.

In late 1966, the game was up. Scolnick pleaded guilty to federal bankruptcy-fraud charges and got authorities to go light on his father-in-law and some of his associates. He was sentenced to five years and began serving time at the Lewisburg (Pa.) federal penitentiary. While in prison he went on a medically supervised diet and dropped about 200 pounds.

There were a dozen state crimes hanging over his head. Philadelphia's crack First Assistant District Attorney Richard Sprague was digging into the whole mess. Scolnick had never before been in prison and felt that he could not survive in the tough environment. He was willing to become a very talkative stool pigeon to avoid more time.

Sprague wanted someone of "star value" from Scolnick, and The Fat Man produced Harry Karafin and a scandal rarely matched in modern newspaper history. The star investigative reporter of the Philadelphia Inquirer was actually a ruthless, rapacious shakedown artist. Like a good investigator, the reporter would ferret-out the wrongdoings and unethical practices of businessmen, bankers, labor organizations and con men, including Scolnick. But he used this information to extort money or merchandise with the threat of a newspaper exposé. A startling number of apparently legitimate businesspeople were paying Karafin to walk away from his typewriter. In many cases, they paid a healthy monthly fee to the reporter for "public relations" services. At Karafin's trial, Sprague estimated that the weasel-like reporter had pocketed $250,000 in shakedown money.

One of Karafin's blackmail victims was none other than bankruptcy-fraud wizard Big Cherry. But Scolnick, being Scolnick, had soon finagled his way from victim to partner in the shakedown racket. Scolnick claimed it was he who suggested the public relations ruse. During Karafin's 1968 trial one victim who paid $10,000 and still got bad publicity in The Inquirer, said the extortion threats came from Scolnick while Karafin just sat nearby and grinned.

Scolnick claimed a former assistant district attorney who headed the fraud unit tipped Karafin off to new cases that could be extorted. The man was investigated and cleared. Scolnick also charged that he was extorted by a top detective in the DA's office who was investigating his bankruptcy-fraud activities. He said he paid the man $5,000 to hold back incriminating evidence. The detective was fired but cleared at his trial. The jury accepted the defense argument that the Fat Felon was a brazen liar trying to get even with the dedicated investigator who sent him to prison.

But Scolnick was providing so much good information that he was transferred from Lewisburg to the Philadelphia Detention Center. Almost daily, he was driven to the District Attorney's office where he was questioned by a host of local, state and federal law enforcement officials. Even Canada had questions for The Fat Man. He provided at least 2,000 hours of interviews.

The star canary was given special privileges during this period, including evening visits to his Cherry Hill home before being returned to jail. His information obviously pleased Sprague and DA Arlen Specter because they recommended that he be allowed to plead guilty to a variety of state charges with the sentences running concurrent with his federal time. Part of the deal was 30 years of probation with the threat that he would serve all three decades if he ever returned to his old ways and broke the law. He was released in May 1970 after 44 months of incarceration. The rotund canary was apparently broke because he couldn't pay a $5,000 federal fine that would have sprung him earlier.

For a brief period, Scolnick worked in his brother's delicatessen. He gave talks on prison reform to clubs and organizations. He appeared on television and radio talk shows and signed a book deal with author Robert H. Adleman.

If anything, the book proved the master scam-man was also a master raconteur, full of charm, wit and color. Writing in the third-person, author Adleman confessed that "his respect for the Fat Man's total lack of hypocrisy was ripening into affection." The book quotes at length an array of honest folk—including a prison warden and a prison priest—who had also developed a respect and affection for Big Cherry. In press interviews, Scolnick declared he could never survive in the prison environment and the fear of 30 years behind bars would guarantee his sincere conversion.

Seventeen months after leaving the slammer, the con man's fleshy face filled the cover of the October 1971 issue of Philadelphia Magazine. Inside was an article entitled "Cherry Hill Fats Rides Again."

The story was a lengthy exposé of Scolnick's new business interest, a franchise operation for a coupon book called the "Golden Book of Values." Perhaps it was a legitimate business but it had all the earmarks of a scam and some of his old cohorts in crime were deeply involved. Big Cherry backed out of the coupon book business with amazing haste, explaining he was only a consultant without any major involvement.

Before his death at age 46, he told an interviewer, "Deals are constantly going through my hands. I can make any kind of deal. But you gotta be careful—there are so many crooks around. You can't trust anybody."

Psychotic shoemaker Joseph Kallinger and his son Michael operated as a father-son crime team.

CHAPTER 14

A Warm Father/Son Relationship
Joe Kallinger

The public first heard the name "Joseph Kallinger" in 1972 when he was arrested and convicted of beating and torturing his own kids. The cops said he even branded his daughter's rear end with a hot spatula.

A year later the Marquis de Sade becomes Mister Rodgers when the kids recant, say they made up the whole torture story. The mousy Kensington shoemaker simply smiles a saintly smile and allows that kids will be kids.

Six months pass and darn if the guy and his kids aren't in the news again. This time crazy, mixed-up Joe Kallinger Jr., age 14, is found dead under a pile of rubble where they are demolishing buildings for The Gallery in Center City. A real tragedy. Then we learn the guy has a load of insurance on the kid and the insurance people are balking. We wonder what the heck is going on. Another six months go by, and there's Joe and one of his kids in the newspapers again! This time it's really incredible. The cops have charged the shoemaker and his 13-year-old son, Michael, with a three-state rampage of burglary, robbery, rape, terror and finally the murder of a woman in a small town in northern New Jersey. A father/son crime team. Weird. Really weird!

It was so bizarre that when Flora Rheta Schreiber, author of the 1973 best seller, *Sybil,* saw the story about the pair in The New York Times, she remembered that "it just leapt off the pages at me." Six years of daily conversation between the intellectual author and the crazed murderer resulted in the 1983 psycho-biography *The Shoemaker.* This book never approached the success of *Sybil,* but it is one the most thorough, chilling and stomach-churning studies of the psychopathic mind ever published.

The Shoemaker was unusual in another way. Kallinger held nothing back from his extremely sympathetic biographer. The author became a mother figure to the schizophrenic killer. To "Mom Flora," Kallinger confessed—as police suspected—that he did, indeed, kill his son Joey with Michael's aid. But he also confessed to a chilling murder of a 10-year-old boy whose death police had never linked to Kallinger.

Schreiber possessed a true believer's faith in psychiatry and in her own abilities to discern profound psychological meanings in Kallinger's twisted thoughts and behavior.

Kallinger's insanity, she declares, all harkened back to "an unloving and grotesquely abnormal childhood." He was the bastard child of a Jewish mother and an Italian-American father. (Schreiber dug out this information and even tracked down the birth mother.) He was adopted at birth by Stephan and Anna Kallinger, childless Austrian immigrants who ran a shoe-repair shop in grimy, industrial Kensington.

Cold, unloving, rigid and eccentric, the Kallingers were at once over-protective and emotionally aloof from their adopted child. Forbidden to play with other children, little Joseph's mission was to learn the cobbler's trade and to be grateful to his adoptive parents who wanted an heir to care for them in old age. According to Schreiber's lay analysis, the boy retreated into his own fantasy world.

The puritanical Kallingers got it into their heads that the boy was sexually precocious at age five when he pulled down the dress of a little girl. When he asked what "fuck" meant he was flogged with a leather strap, beaten with a wooden spoon and locked in the house for a week. At eight he was jumped by a gang and forced to participate in a homosexual act. When his father caught Joe stealing some coins, he burned Joe's hands. When he asked Mom Kallinger's permission to join a school trip to the zoo, she replied, "You're not here to play; you're here to repair shoes." When the boy persisted, good old Mom hit Joe on the head with a steel tool. Her pet name for little Joe was "dummkopf."

Pop-psychologist Schreiber says Joe was obsessed with blood and knives. She traces this to a childhood hernia operation. Kallinger told the author he could never have sex without a knife in his hand—usually a closed penknife. By 12, he had the urge to castrate other boys. He was also a pyromaniac.

By age 15 Joe was so warped, his adoptive parents felt they had to pad-lock their bedroom door from the inside to protect themselves from their strange son. They had succeeded in creating their own Frankenstein.

At 16, Joe left home, married and fathered two children. His wife soon realized that Joe was off his rocker and ran off with another man. Neither she nor the kids had further contact with Kallinger. They were about the only people in Kallinger's life who refused to talk with Schreiber.

The way Schreiber sees it, a major theme in Kallinger's life was abandonment. His birth mother, the Kallingers, his wife and kids had all abandoned Joe. So when he married a second time, he wanted a large, loving and dependent family that would never abandon him. New wife Betty was an ideal mate. Docile and none too perceptive, she never realized her husband was batty.

Kallinger fathered another five kids with Betty. We learn that Joe had an incestuous relationship with his daughter Mary Jo when she was 11. From the shoemaker's point of view, it was a tender and sweet father-daughter relationship. With a psychotic father and passive mother, not surprisingly, the three older kids ran wild. To bring them under control, Joe resorted to the beatings and torture that resulted in his seven months behind bars.

After his release, business practically died in the Kallinger shoe shop. In order to bring some money into the family coffers, the kids agreed to recant their tales of terror.

Kallinger's insanity deepened. He purchased an abandoned house in the neighborhood and made the kids dig a 20-foot-deep hole in the basement. He would descend into the pit at night with a candle. There, writes Schreiber, Kallinger chanted and "conducted assorted rituals with masturbation and defecation as elements of the ritual."

Then Kallinger started receiving orders from God to massacre all of mankind. He started with 10-year-old third-grader Jose Collazo. Kallinger and his son Michael met the child in front of a neighborhood recreation center and promised him money for help in moving some boxes. The boy was led to an abandoned rug factory, stripped and bound. He died of suffocation when Kallinger stuffed socks into the boy's throat as a gag. An innocent black man was arrested for the crime and released about two weeks later—but not before a vengeful mob destroyed his house.

Michael assisted his father in every crime. Schreiber says Kallinger couldn't act without Michael. Her explanation: "Michael was Joe's courage. Michael was the inner child of the past. As a child, Joe didn't have the courage to do the things Michael did, but he had the desire."

Murder Victim Two was his own troubled and troublesome son Joey, a nasty delinquent and a homosexual. Kallinger engineered two failed murder attempts. One involved sending Joey into a trailer at a construction site with bottles of gasoline and matches to set it on fire. It was the kind of fun the Kallinger boys loved. Michael wedged a box against the door hoping to trap Joey inside. But the kid broke out, never suspecting the caper was meant as his death trap.

Next, dad and the two kids went exploring at a Market Street demolition site where they found an entrance to a flooded basement. In the basement, they found a ladder. On the pretext of having his photo taken, Joey was chained and locked to the ladder. Then it was pushed into the pool of filthy water in the basement. When the 14-year-old stopped breathing, Joe and Michael removed the chains and locks, and that night Kallinger reported Joey missing. When the body was found 11 days later by workmen, it seemed like an accidental death. Except there were three insurance policies on the boy's life, all with double-indemnity clauses for accidental death.

Next came the remarkable six-week father/son crime spree. Starting in late November 1974, the pair ranged from Maryland to Harrisburg to North Jersey. While they accumulated an impressive haul of cash and jewelry, there was no planning and no real reason for the crimes other than Kallinger's growing insanity and blood lust. Michael just thought it was great fun.

Kallinger and the boy would simply board a Greyhound bus, get off in a place they had never before seen and select a house. Armed with knives and a gun, they would rob and terrorize the occupants.

In one of their first crimes, in Lindenwold, N.J., the pair simply knocked on a door. Seeing a boy and a man, the female occupant unlocked her door, and the pair pushed their way inside. Kallinger would strip and blindfold female victims, terrorize them with a knife and attempt rape, but always failed to get an erection. Michael frequently asked if he could have sex with a victim, but Joe was against it.

In a comfortable suburb of Harrisburg, Kallinger and Michael entered a house where four middle-aged matrons were gathering for an afternoon bridge party. As each woman arrived, she was captured and bound. The victims were moved about the house and threatened with a knife. Kallinger told his biographer that at this point he was deep into hallucinations. He was seeing his own double killing and slashing. At other times a floating, disembodied head commanded him to kill. Because of the hallucinations, he was under the impression that he had slaughtered and mutilated the women at the bridge party. In fact, he had only inflicted a minor nick with his knife on one woman.

In Dumont, N.J., the pair invaded a house where Kallinger tied a woman to her bed and forced her to perform oral sex. This time he relented and allowed Michael to try his hand at rape.

On January 8, 1975 the pair's ramblings took them to Leonia, N.J., not far from New York City. In midafternoon they entered a house. At gunpoint they stripped and bound two young women, a small boy and an elderly female. Soon three visitors arrived at the house—two women and a husky man. They, too, were captured at gunpoint, tied and blindfolded but not stripped naked.

Then a young woman knocked on the door; Kallinger let her in with a welcoming smile; now the pair had eight captives. Apparently, the man of the house had recently suffered a heart attack and was in the hospital. Friends and family were gathering to offer support to the wife.

The last visitor was a 21-year-old nurse, Maria Fasching, an attractive and spirited woman who was less fearful than the other hog-tied victims scattered about the house. "Get out now, both of you! You don't belong here," she shouted.

At first the nurse refused to allow herself to be tied and gagged. According to Kallinger, it was "the killer look" in Michael's eyes—he held the gun—that sapped her will to resist. Kallinger took Maria to the basement where the lone man was tied up. Kallinger told Schreiber that at this point his hallucinations were racing at full gallop. He ordered the nurse "to chew off" the man's penis. The woman refused, saying she preferred to die. In a blind psychotic rage, Kallinger stabbed the young woman to death with his hunting knife.

About the same time, one of the upstairs hostages broke loose and dashed into the street yelling for help. Michael led Kallinger from the house. They made a mad dash through town, tossing away their loot, the gun and the hunting knife. In a small park, Kallinger took off his coat and shirt and started washing the blood from his hands and the shirt in a rain puddle. Then he discarded the shirt, which contained a laundry mark and the name "Kallinger" stamped on the inside of the collar. Joe and Michael hopped a bus to New York and took a train back to Philly. It took police a few days to locate the dry cleaner in Philadelphia. On January 17, 1975, a party of FBI supported by police from New Jersey, Maryland and Philadelphia raided the Kallinger home and arrested father and son.

Michael was handled by juvenile authorities and eventually placed in a foster home. For the shoemaker, there was a series of trials. His lawyers used an insanity defense. Joe helped out by chirping like a bird in the courtroom. Better yet, he testified that he was 1,000 years old, spoke directly to God and had once lived as a butterfly.

It was during these trials that Schreiber entered Kallinger's life and never left it. He signed a contract with the author to be paid 12.5 percent of the book's royalties in return for his complete cooperation.

Kallinger did, indeed, open up. For Schreiber, a person who relished the role of pop-psychiatrist, Joe Kallinger was a dream come true. He revealed everything and never stopped talking.

Following the trials and convictions, Kallinger would call Schreiber collect up to three times a day from Pennsylvania's Farview State Hospital for the Criminally Insane. The author's monthly telephone bills ran upward of $1,000. Kallinger sent the author Mother's Day cards and often referred to the unwed, childless author playfully as "Mom Flora."

He couldn't have asked for a more supportive and understanding friend. Schreiber would adamantly proclaim her belief that "Joe is not bad. He is sick. . . . He has many likable qualities. He has a good mind. He is very intelligent. I sometimes forget that he is a convicted murderer; there is no sense that he is a criminal. I regard this as an illness, rather than criminality."

Indeed, there is not the slightest hint of condemnation of Kallinger in the book. Whether it's sex with an 11-year-old daughter, murdering a son or terrorizing suburban housewives, the book's viewpoint is that of the psychotic subject, not the victims'.

Schreiber was livid when Kallinger was tried and convicted for the murders of Joey and Jose Collazo after the book was released. She was equally upset anytime there was a threat that Kallinger might be transferred from the therapeutic setting of Farview to a state prison.

Kallinger often parroted the author's ideas and words; he began writing poetry and started his own book. Schreiber's assertion that abandonment was a constant theme in the shoemaker's life led her to declare, "If I were to abandon him, that would be the final and worst abandonment. It's a tremendous responsibility and a strain."

Schreiber died at age 70 in November 1988. A suicidal Kallinger died in prison on March 26, 1996 of natural causes. The death of the once infamous shoemaker went unnoticed by the local news media for six weeks.

Newspaper heir John S. Knight III (bottom right) died at the hands
of Salvatore Soli (top left), Steven Maleno (top right)
and Isais "Felix" Melendez (bottom left).

CHAPTER 15

A Not So Gay Life
John S. Knight III

It was certainly one of the most sensational Philadelphia murders of the 1970s. It dominated local news and stirred national attention because of the prominence of the victim and the titillating revelations that surfaced about "the secret life" of John S. Knight III.

Looked at from a different angle, the slaying of the young millionaire in his expensively furnished Rittenhouse Square apartment was as unplanned and opportunistic as a gang of punks rolling a drunk in a North Philly alley.

The 30-year-old victim was heir-apparent of the Knight-Ridder newspaper chain. The combined circulation of its 35 newspapers made the chain the largest in the nation. The young man who would one day own the controlling shares in this sprawling enterprise was a Harvard and Oxford graduate, a collector and connoisseur of modern art; a gourmet; a fit athlete, hunter and scuba diver. He enjoyed the good life but impressed those around him as intellectual, competent and hard-working.

Knight never knew his father who was killed in World War II just two months before his birth. It fell to his grandfather, newspaper tycoon John Shively Knight, to play a major role in the boy's rearing and education.

Knight was to inherit his grandfather's $90 million in company stock and was being groomed to take over the reins of control from the 81-year-old patriarch. During his high school and college years Knight began his apprenticeship by working summers at newspapers in the chain. After completing his education, Knight spent five years learning the business in a variety of positions at the Detroit Free Press, where he distinguished himself as a reporter and editorial writer. In addition to winning two journalism awards, Knight received a tip in 1972 concerning the mental health problems that led Democratic vice presidential candidate Sen. Thomas Eagleton to withdraw from the ticket.

In late 1974, Knight transferred to Philadelphia where the chain owned both the Inquirer and Daily News. Apparently, much could be learned at the lively, unconventional Daily News, where Knight was taken on as a $350-a-week night copy editor. Everyone at the tabloid knew that Knight was the Chief's grandson, but he played it low-key and sought no special treatment.

Certainly, a copy editor with more than $1 million in his bank account enjoys a totally different life-style away from work than his colleagues. But no one at the newspaper suspected how really different Knight's life-style was away from the grungy newsroom. The pre-dawn events of December 7, 1975, would reveal Knight's surprising secret life to the world.

It was the weekend and Knight was busy entertaining houseguests. A dear Harvard chum, Dr. John McKinnon, and his wife, Rosemary, were visiting from New Haven, where McKinnon was then a resident in psychiatry; his wife was a British-born psychologist. The two men had been roommates, and the newsman was given best man honors at the couple's wedding.

That evening Knight played gracious host—a role he relished. He treated the McKinnons; his own date, a woman who worked at a bank; and Daily News Managing Editor Paul Janensch and his wife to a sumptuous dinner at La Truffe restaurant. It was a four-hour feast centered around pheasants that Knight had bagged on a hunting trip in South Dakota. Fine wines and good liquor flowed freely.

Shortly after midnight, the Janensches and Knight's companion left together. The McKinnons returned with Knight to his spacious 23rd-floor apartment at The Dorchester where the friends continued to chat about old times over more drinks.

In another part of town a different gathering of friends was also up late. They were smoking marijuana, shooting Methedrine into their arms and drinking beer rather than scotch. Five people were gathered in the South Philly rowhouse of baker and ex-convict Joe Paolucci.

The group included Salvatore Soli, 37, a nasty, bantam-sized South Philly drug addict and minor hoodlum. The news media would say Soli's police record included 50 arrests with five cases pending. Soli had brought two females to the gathering. One was his girlfriend Donna Marie DePaul, 20, who would later admit using drugs daily from age 17. She had been arrested only the year before for selling meth to an undercover agent.

The other female with Soli was a new acquaintance: Linda Mary Wells was a shapely 18-year-old blonde who had recently run away from home near Syracuse. Her good looks had landed her a job as a stripper at one of the nation's last old-style burlesque houses, the Troc, near 10th and Arch. Linda—whose gimmick was her girl-next-door looks— was bumping and grinding under the stage name "Tarri." Rounding out the party were Paolucci and Steven Maleno, 25, another South Philly junkie.

None had ever heard the name John S. Knight III. But that would change when a sixth person arrived. In order to pay the rent, Paolucci had taken in a roommate: Isais "Felix" Melendez. Some time before midnight Melendez arrived home and was introduced to Soli, Maleno and the girls. Unlike the others, Felix was Hispanic. He was very handsome in a delicate way that made him attractive to both young girls and gay men.

Melendez joined in the pot smoking and meth use. Soli wanted more drugs, but no one had money. Those at the party said their new companion offered a solution. Melendez said he knew "this fag John," a rich guy living on Rittenhouse Square who would be easy to rip off.

Soli immediately pressured Melendez to telephone the potential mark. Dr. McKinnon would remember his conversation with Knight being interrupted about 1 a.m. by a phone call. Knight spoke softly, but his guest remembered him saying, "I can't see you tonight. I have houseguests." Knight slyly told McKinnon it was someone who procured women for him. McKinnon felt a bit embarrassed by the explanation.

Soli reportedly pressed Melendez to call later. Melendez got dressed in a flamboyant "superfly" outfit and at 3 a.m. called again. In a fruity voice Melendez cooed, "John, I love you." The others snickered while Melendez cajoled and expressed his affection. After the call Melendez, Soli and Maleno left for The Dorchester. What happened at Knight's apartment is not fully known. But the chilling courtroom testimony of John and Rosemary McKinnon of what followed can accurately be characterized as surreal and nightmarish.

The couple had retired to a guest bedroom. Knight probably opened his door for Melendez and the other two pushed in behind. Soli had a gun. There was a scuffle with Knight who was probably in better shape than any of the intruders. But Knight was overpowered and hog-tied with ropes, and gagged with his own expensive neckties.

The trio then searched the apartment, which had numerous rooms and closets. The intruders soon discovered the two guests asleep. McKinnon was sleeping so deeply, the trio decided to leave him alone. Rosemary McKinnon was allowed to wrap herself in a blanket and was hustled into another room. At one point during her two-hour ordeal she saw John Knight on his bedroom floor trussed-up and moaning.

Soli bound the woman but spent a good deal of time with her, sometimes threatening or making obscene remarks and suggestions. Melendez, high on drugs, tramped around the apartment carrying Knight's diving knife, a menacing harpoon gun and sometimes a hunting rifle. From time to time, Melendez would turn the stereo set on and off. The whole scene was more than a bit surreal.

The place was ransacked, and loot believed valuable stuffed into suit-cases. At some point a neighbor in the apartment below Knight called the front desk to complain of thumping noises. The night attendant knocked on the door and requested that the noise be kept down. Eventually Soli and Maleno left the apartment. Melendez stayed behind and unbound Mrs. McKinnon and brought her into Knight's bedroom. "There was a slight sound. I'm not sure what it was, but Melendez was startled," the woman testified at Soli's trial. She used that instant to jump on her captive, snatch the rifle and dash into the guest room where her husband was still sleeping soundly. She managed to shake him awake and blurt out what was going on.

"I woke up to the bizarre sight of my wife with a rifle in her hand," McKinnon recalled. "She was very frightened and anxious and talking very fast. In the hallway I saw a young man who turned out to be Felix Melendez pointing a speargun at my chest. I said, 'Put that down. You don't need that, you idiot.'"

Then McKinnon slammed the bedroom door, threw on some clothes and went out to confront Melendez. He found the young intruder standing on Knight's bed holding the speargun, shaking with fear and screaming, "I didn't do it to him." Knight was bound, lying facedown and not moving. Melendez dashed passed McKinnon. The physician chased him into the hallway, knocked him to the floor, and ordered him to stay put.

In the meantime, Rosemary McKinnon tried to call police but found the telephone was dead. She decided to go to the lobby to seek help. Just as she entered the elevator, Melendez dashed into the corridor and jumped into the elevator with the woman. The skinny, sweet-faced intruder held a knife.

On the trip down, Mrs. McKinnon grabbed the knife blade and received minor cuts to her fingers and a nick on her chest. She dashed out on the third floor and down the fire stairs to the lobby where she alerted the desk clerk.

Back in the apartment, McKinnon found his friend's face wrapped in at least 15 neckties. Knight wasn't breathing and there was no pulse. McKinnon tried mouth-to-mouth resuscitation and smashed his fist into Knight's chest in an attempt to start his heart. He soon realized his old college mate was dead.

An autopsy showed the victim had been stabbed four times in the back and once in the chest. In addition, he had been struck in the head with a blunt instrument. Knight's body was identified by Daily News Editor Gil Spencer who had been on the job for only two months and was now facing a terrible mess.

The murder was more than an unexpected shock at the Daily News and

The Inquirer: It presented some delicate decisions for writers and editors. The victim wasn't just any rich guy; he was the beloved grandson of the Editorial Chairman of the Knight-Ridder chain. Yet there was no way to avoid the homosexual angle of a very sensational story.

The first-day Daily News story declared that Mrs. McKinnon believed "from the conversations at least one of the assailants appeared to be a homosexual. She also told police that conversations among the intruders indicated they believed Knight was homosexual."

The newspaper went on to say that "detectives interviewed several known homosexuals and homosexual procurers. . . . Among the effects police removed from Knight's apartment were several dozen photographs of nude young men. . . . Chief Inspector Joseph Golden, commander of the detective bureau, refused comment on the homosexual implications in the case."

As ticklish as the lurid story was for the two newspapers, it was also "great copy." Viewing it as a newsman, John Praksta, retired Daily News night editor and Knight's immediate boss, muses, "It was one of the best, most dramatic local murders I had seen in 37 years. For almost a month we had a fresh, legitimate angle every day." No one at the News suspected Knight's homosexuality. "I saw him at parties with women," says Praksta. "He dated the daughter of a man who worked in the photo department. I guess his dating her was a cover.

"Several times he went to New York City for a weekend with a girl-friend," Praksta recalled. "He was supposed to work on Sunday nights. But he'd call from New York and say he couldn't make it. There was always some weird incident. He'd say his girlfriend got robbed at their hotel, or something like that. I guess he was with that Billy Sage."

Just 12 hours after the news of the murder broke, 20-year-old Billy Sage arrived in Philadelphia from Detroit. Tall and baby-faced with shoulder-length blond hair, Sage declared himself Knight's lover and "best friend" during the past five years. He identified the key to a footlocker in Knight's apartment containing a variety of pornography: lewd magazines, sexual devices, tape recordings, and lewd photographs of both homosexual and heterosexual varieties. Sage then flew off to Columbus, Ga., to attend Knight's burial. The family was less than delighted by the sudden appearance of the strange, bisexual "best friend" and firmly denied Sage's request to be a pallbearer.

It would seem that Knight, Sage and Melendez all shared a rather confused and troublesome bisexual identity. Sage told reporters he married about the same time Knight left Detroit for Philadelphia. He said his wealthy friend paid for his honeymoon in England and sent gifts of cash regularly. Despite the marriage, the pair continued to see each other.

Melendez was not only a male prostitute, he was also very popular with young women. A year prior to the Knight murder, Melendez fathered a child and reportedly offered to marry the girl; her father vetoed that idea. Melendez's brother was shocked and disbelieving: They were raised in a religious family. Their father was a Pentecostal minister, the former pastor of a church in North Philly, who had recently returned to Puerto Rico with most of the family.

As for John Knight III, even McKinnon said it never entered his mind that the man he knew so well might be bisexual or homosexual. Colleagues at the Detroit Free Press who thought they knew John Knight were astounded to learn of his double life. Newspaper friends there said Knight dated many women, enjoyed the raunchy fun of go-go bars, and purchased the services of female prostitutes.

The contents of the diaries found in The Dorchester were never disclosed, but enough material leaked to reveal a man with a large sexual appetite perversely drawn to sordid women and bad boy prostitutes, known as "chicken-hawks." The diaries also revealed a tortured soul plagued by guilt but believing he would someday overcome his homosexuality and marry a woman of his own social class.

All the pressures, insecurities and excessive drinking led Knight to seek psychiatric help, both in Detroit and Philly. Friends in Detroit said Knight spent more than $10,000 in one year on daily consultations with a psychiatrist.

The newspapers described "a massive search" for the killers. There were a lot of leads for police to work with including Knight's personal telephone list and excellent composite sketches of the three suspects based on descriptions supplied by the McKinnons.

Scores of homosexuals in the city's "gay ghetto," centered on 15th and Spruce streets, were questioned by police. Some reportedly recognized the sketch of Melendez and a few would later recall seeing Melendez and Knight together. On December 11—four days after the murder—police announced the names and released the photos of the three suspects. Photos of Melendez, Soli and Maleno nicely matched the sketches of the police artist. Robbery was the motive behind the murder, said Golden.

The next day's headlines blared sensational new developments. Hours after the suspects' names were released, Melendez's corpse was found on the grounds of a South Jersey golf course with bullet holes in his head and body. And just hours before the body was discovered, Steven Maleno surrendered to Philadelphia detectives.

The Pine Valley Country Club is the kind of place Knight might have frequented. It is one of the most challenging and exclusive golf courses in the world—so exclusive that the golf course is an independent municipality with a population of about 10 employees who live on the grounds. A caddy spotted the corpse under a pine tree. At first it was thought that Melendez had been dead only a few hours. It was later learned that the body had been lying in the cold December weather for three days.

The investigation was moving swiftly. Several items taken from Knight's apartment were found in a sewer a few yards from the Paolucci house. Police learned that Soli and two women had stayed the past few nights at motels in Mount Ephraim and Bellmawr, N.J.

Maleno was in custody, Melendez was dead. The hunt was on for Soli. His mother tearfully pleaded on television news for her son to contact the family. Seven days after the Knight murder a pretty but frightened blonde stopped a Miami cop and declared, "I know something about the murders in Philadelphia."

It was stripper Linda Mary Wells, and she led cops to a $10-a-night motel where she had been staying with Soli and Donna DePaul. Tough guy Soli had shaved off his moustache and dyed his hair a weird shade of strawberry blond, bordering on international orange. The trio did not fight extradition and was soon transported back to Philadelphia. The women and Paolucci were all talking to police and basically telling the same tale that started with the gathering at Paolucci's house and the decision to rob Knight.

They said Soli and Maleno returned after sunrise with the loot, including checkbooks, jewelry, rings and watches. Both men indicated that Melendez had killed Knight. They were furious over the unnecessary violence. Had the caper been handled properly, Knight might have never reported the incident for fear of revealing his secret life.

Donna DePaul would later testify that Soli said, "That stupid kid got us into a lot of trouble." Paolucci quoted Melendez as admitting, "I screwed up. I cut a guy." The girls recalled Soli and Maleno venting their rage on the young Hispanic.

Hours after the murder, Soli took the girls to a motel in South Jersey. The entire gang gathered there later that night. The four men and two women piled into two cars and began cruising Camden County. They halted on a rural road. Maleno and Melendez got out and walked away to bury some incriminating bloody clothes. Those waiting in the cars heard shots. Maleno returned alone. He reportedly said that Felix had decided to hide out somewhere else. Soli and the girls spent another two nights in South Jersey motels before taking off for Miami in a car that broke down in South Carolina. They completed the trip by bus.

With Wells' tip to the Miami police, the investigation was essentially over. In fact, Soli gave a confession in Miami, but later disavowed it. The two women were charged with aiding and abetting in Soli's escape; a judge later tossed out the charges.

Less than six months after Knight's slaying, Soli was tried for the murder. District Attorney F. Emmett Fitzpatrick handled the high-profile case himself. Soli was represented by the slick and wily Nino Tinari, who would later have his own troubles with the law.

Donna DePaul and both McKinnons testified for the prosecution. Tinari built his defense on the assertion that Melendez went berserk and killed Knight after Soli and Maleno had left The Dorchester. He called no defense witnesses. Soli's very ill and very distraught mother attended the trial in a wheelchair.

In his closing to the jury, Fitzpatrick declared, "Salvatore Soli was the captain of the team. He was the quarterback, the man who made each and every decision, the leader of a band of Vikings wreaking terror all over Rittenhouse Square." Minutes after the DA's summation, Soli's mother suffered an apparent heart attack and was rushed to a hospital. The jury convicted Soli of first-degree murder and related charges but split on the death penalty, resulting in a life sentence.

Shortly after Soli's conviction, Maleno pleaded guilty to the Knight murder and entered a second guilty plea to the murder of Melendez. On the day of his sentencing in Camden County, Maleno had a sudden change of heart, shouting at the judge. "I didn't kill anyone in Philadelphia. I didn't kill anyone in New Jersey." It was too late. Paolucci confessed his involvement in the Melendez slaying and was given a four-to-five-year prison sentence.

The Knight murder contained many elements of Greek tragedy. In fact, the highly educated newsman sometimes quoted lines in classical Greek—with translation—for colleagues if the phrase was apropos of the subject at hand. But the young man with so much intellect, sophistication and potential found the most sordid street-life irresistible. Both male and female hustlers had visited his posh apartment. Perhaps it was hubris to believe he could play in the sewers and escape the stink and danger.

BIBLIOGRAPHY

Adleman, Robert H. *Alias Big Cherry: The Confessions of a Master Criminal.* New York: Dial Press, 1973.

Bell, Arthur. *Kings Don't Mean a Thing: The John Knight Murder Case.* New York: William Morrow & Co., 1978.

Geyer, Frank P. *The Holmes-Pitezel Case: A History of the Greatest Crime of the Century.* Philadelphia: Publishers Union, 1896.

Lewis, Arthur H. *The Worlds of Chippy Patterson.* New York: Harcourt Brace & Co., 1960.

McCaffery, Peter. *When Bosses Ruled Philadelphia.* University Park, Pa.: The Pennsylvania State University Press, 1993.

Mann, William. *The Trial of Anton Probst for the Murder of Christopher Deering and Family at Philadelphia.* Philadelphia: T.B Peterson & Brothers, 1867.

Unknown author. *The Life, Confession and Atrocious Crime of Anton Probst.* Philadelphia: Barclay & Co, 1866.

Zierold, Norman. *Little Charley Ross.* Boston: Little, Brown & Company, 1967.